S0-BDP-154

# Arguing for Atheism

'Le Poidevin's *Arguing for Atheism* is the best recent introduction to the philosophy of religion. Le Poidevin writes in a clear and engaging manner, without sacrifice of conceptual precision or argumentative depth. One way his book is distinguished from standard introductions to the philosophy of religion is the inclusion of some recent developments.... Le Poidevin gives a fair evaluation of both atheism and theism and his book is eminently suitable for courses on philosophy of religion...He does not merely recapitulate familiar ideas but introduces original and plausible arguments of his own. I would highly recommend this book to students and professors alike.'

*Quentin Smith, Western Michigan University*

In *Arguing for Atheism*, Robin Le Poidevin addressses the question of whether theism – the view that there is a personal, transcendent creator of the universe – solves the deepest mysteries of existence. Philosophical defences of theism have often been based on the the idea that it explains things which atheistic approaches cannot: for example, why the universe exists, and how there can be objective moral values.

The main contention of *Arguing for Atheism* is that the reverse is true: that in fact theism fails to explain many things it claims to, while atheism can explain some of the things it supposedly leaves mysterious. It is also argued that religion need not depend on belief in God.

Designed as a text for university courses in the philosophy of religion and metaphysics, this book's accessible style and numerous explanations of important philosophical concepts and positions will also make it attractive to the general reader.

**Robin Le Poidevin** is Senior Lecturer in Philosophy at the University of Leeds. He is the author of *Change, Cause and Contradiction: A Defence of the Tenseless Theory of Time* (1991) and co-editor, with Murray MacBeath, of *The Philosophy of Time* (1993).

# Arguing for Atheism

## An introduction to the philosophy of religion

Robin Le Poidevin

BL
51
.L355
1996

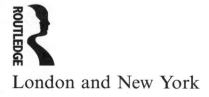

London and New York

First published 1996
by Routledge
11 New Fetter Lane, London EC4P 4EE

Simultaneously published in the USA and Canada
by Routledge
29 West 35th Street, New York, NY 10001

*Routledge is an International Thomson Publishing company*

© 1996 Robin Le Poidevin

Typeset in Times by Routledge
Printed and bound in Great Britain by
Biddles Ltd, Guildford and King's Lynn

All rights reserved. No part of this book may be reprinted or
reproduced or utilised in any form or by any electronic,
mechanical, or other means, now known or hereafter
invented, including photocopying and recording, or in any
information storage or retrieval system, without permission in
writing from the publishers.

*British Library Cataloguing in Publication Data*
A catalogue record for this book is available from the British
Library

*Library of Congress Cataloguing in Publication Data*
Le Poidevin, Robin, 1962–
Arguing for atheism: an introduction to the philosophy of
religion/Robin Le Poidevin.
Includes bibliographical references and index.
1. Religion – Philosophy. 2. Atheism. I. Title.
BL51.L355 1996
211'.8–dc20                    96–3431
                               CIP

ISBN 0–415–09337–6 (hbk)
ISBN 0–415–09338–4 (pbk)

*For my parents, Roy and Barbara,*
*and my children, Tom and Sam*

# Contents

# Illustrations

## FIGURES

## TABLES

# Preface

I have tried to write a book suitable for use as a text in second- or third-year undergraduate philosophy of religion and metaphysics courses. I have also tried, while aiming at a degree of argumentative depth, to make it accessible to those with no previous acquaintance with philosophy, by defining important terms and theories, both in the text and in a glossary at the end. Much of the same ground is covered as would be covered by a conventional introduction to the philosophy of religion, such as the classic arguments for the existence of God, the problem of evil, and the relationship between morality and religion. However, the introduction offered here is unconventional in a number of respects. Whereas most introductions to a subject tend to remain neutral, to display positions and arguments rather than to defend or attack them, this book builds a case for atheism, understood as the rejection of the independent existence of a personal creator of the universe. And, whereas the chapters of introductions are usually almost entirely autonomous, the chapters of this book lead from one to another. I have nevertheless tried to give the chapters a degree of autonomy, so that it is possible to select some but not others for teaching purposes.

Needless to say, the case for atheism presented here is very incomplete. Theism has many resources at its disposal, as I hope to make clear. My aim has been to provide a starting-point for discussion, to provoke debate rather than to silence opposition.

As well as a particular direction, the book also has a distinctive emphasis: on *metaphysical* issues in religion. For reasons that I articulate in the Introduction, I believe that there is a very close connection between religion, especially theistic religion, and metaphysics. So the issues discussed here are presented as metaphysical issues, concerning causation, time, necessity, ontology, and so on. What I hope is one of the novel aspects of the book is that disputes that arise in other areas are brought to bear on religious issues. For example, in Chapter 2 I introduce different conceptions of modality and draw out the consequences they have for the ontological argument and the notion of a necessary God. Chapter 4 discusses two theories of probability, and shows how these create difficulties for the probabilistic version of the teleological argument. The nature of time is the subject of the final chapter, in which I discuss the relationship between our views on time and our attitudes towards death. Each chapter, in fact, introduces metaphysical issues, and these are listed below.

Chapter 1: Causation and time
Chapter 2: Possibility and necessity
Chapter 3: Causal explanation
Chapter 4: Probability
Chapter 5: Teleology
Chapter 6: Moral realism
Chapter 7: Determinism
Chapter 8: Fictional objects
Chapter 9: Ontology
Chapter 10: Time and the self

Finally, philosophy of religion courses and texts tend to be dominated by a realist conception of theistic discourse as positing the existence of a transcendent deity, and so as evaluable as true or false. But since a number of 'radical' theologians have rejected this conception, and urged instead what might be described as an instrumentalist view of talk about God, there is an urgent need for philosophical discussion of what I believe to be one of the key religious issues of our times. In Part III I offer a contribution to that debate. I have been sympathetic to the programme of radical theology ever since I had the good fortune, while a research student in Cambridge, to hear at first hand the ideas of Don Cupitt. He has been very influential in my thinking about the philosophy of religion, despite the fact that our philosophical approaches are quite different. Although what is offered here is in the end an atheistic picture, then, it is not an anti-religious one.

*Leeds, November 1995*

# Acknowledgements

I have been helped by many people during the writing of this book. I would particularly like to thank the following:

Kate Meakin, for support and constructively sceptical comments, and for suggesting the title.

Nigel Warburton, for reading through nearly all the typescript and making many helpful and detailed suggestions for improvement.

The late Murray MacBeath, who helped me to see how I should revise an early draft of the first part of the book.

Don Cupitt and Quentin Smith, for helpful comments on the penultimate draft.

Adrian Driscoll, at Routledge, for encouraging me to write the book in the first place, offering advice, and patiently waiting for two years after the original deadline for the final version.

My Department, for granting me study leave in which to write the book.

My colleagues at Leeds, and in particular Jonathan Hodge, Peter Millican, Mark Nelson, Chris Megone and Piers Benn, for illuminating discussions on the philosophy of religion and comments on parts of the book.

The Editor of *Cogito*, and Carfax Publishing Company, for permission to re-use material from two articles, 'Autonomous Agents or God's Automata?' and 'Time, Death and the Atheist', which appear in modified form in this book in Chapters 7 and 10 respectively.

The Editor of *Religious Studies*, and Cambridge University Press, for permission to reuse material from 'Internal and External Questions about God', which appears in modified form in this book in Chapter 9. Full details of these three articles are given below:

'Autonomous Agents or God's Automata? Human Freedom from the Divine Perspective', *Cogito* 9 (1995), pp. 35–41.

'Time, Death and the Atheist', *Cogito* 9 (1995), pp. 145–52.

'Internal and External Questions About God', *Religious Studies* 31 (1995)

The ancient covenant is in pieces; man at last knows that he is alone in the unfeeling immensity of the universe, out of which he emerged only by chance. Neither his destiny nor his duty have been written down. The kingdom above or the darkness below: it is for him to choose.

Jacques Monod, Chance and Necessity

# Introduction

'What a silly thing Love is!' said the Student as he walked away. 'It is not half as useful as Logic, for it does not prove anything, and it is always telling one of things that are not going to happen, and making one believe things that are not true. In fact, it is quite unpractical, and as in this age to be practical is everything, I shall go back to Philosophy, and study Metaphysics.'

So he returned to his room and pulled out a great dusty book, and began to read.

Oscar Wilde, *The Nightingale and the Rose*

Atheism, as presented in this book, is a definite doctrine, and defending it requires one to engage with religious ideas. An *atheist* is one who denies the existence of a personal, transcendent creator of the universe, rather than one who simply lives life without reference to such a being. A *theist* is one who asserts the existence of such a creator. Any discussion of atheism, then, is necessarily a discussion of theism.

I am concerned in this book, not just with religion, but with the *philosophy* of religion, and the argument for atheism presented here is a philosophical argument. Now this may provoke some scepticism. What, it may be asked, has philosophy as an academic discipline to do with the rejection or acceptance of religious belief? They seem poles apart, with belief on the one hand promising to transform our lives through a revelation of our purpose and destiny, and philosophy on the other concerned with abstruse arguments, an activity only for specialists who are wont to mumble to each other in some esoteric language while in pursuit of the incommunicable.

To articulate it in a less polemical way, the objection is that philosophical arguments are beside the point, for, whereas philosophy is concerned with rational justification, religion is a matter not of justification but of faith. There are philosophical arguments for the existence of God, but even the proponents of these arguments, such as Anselm and Descartes, did not necessarily hold that belief should be based on them. Both Anselm and Descartes thought that religious truths were directly revealed by God. The purpose of argument was, therefore, to reinforce, rather than to establish, faith. As such, argument was supplementary rather than essential. More recently, writers have come to see the traditional proofs as invalid, or as making controversial assumptions, and thus as unconvincing. Faith, however, can remain unshaken by this. Philosophical argument is simply *de trop*.

In reply to this objection, I make the following points:

1 Even if no-one, as a matter of fact, has ever based their faith on rational justification, it still remains an interesting question whether such justification could be given.

2 Even if the traditional arguments fail, in the sense that they do not provide conclusive reasons for belief, they highlight some of the perplexities which make religion, and theism in particular, so attractive. For example, it is natural to wonder whether the order in the world bears testimony to the existence of a designer. Theism at least gives the appearance of providing an explanation for such things as the existence of the universe, the emergence of life, and our moral consciousness. So we need to ask, *does* theism provide explanations for these things? This is a philosophical question.

3 Even if it is a mistake to see theism, or some other form of religion, as if it were providing an explanation of anything, still it needs to be shown that this *is* a mistake. One way of doing this would be to show that theism fails as any kind of explanation.

4 Even if justification is irrelevant, we may still wish to know what precisely theism commits us to, what consequences it has. One philosophical argument against theism is that it commits us to unacceptable (including morally unacceptable) beliefs.

5 If religion is immune from philosophical attack, if the question of rational justification simply does not arise in this context, then it is natural to ask whether religious discourse is fact-stating in the way that everyday discourse is. For example, if I say, 'There are no trains running between Settle and Carlisle today', I would normally be taken to be stating a fact, and be expected to be able to justify my remark (or at least to recognise that such a remark could be justified or shown to be mistaken). If I say, 'There is a God', and refuse either to justify my remark or to regard any attempted criticism of it as relevant, then it is a possibility that I am not intending to state a fact about the world at all. At least, there is an issue here, and it is a philosophical one.

I want to argue, then, that philosophy, and in particular that branch of philosophy called 'metaphysics', has an important role to play in the debate about religious belief. But what is metaphysics? Very broadly, metaphysics is concerned with the nature of reality. So, too, of course, is science. But science and metaphysics differ, both in the specificity of the questions they ask and in the methods they use to answer them. Consider the questions which form the chapter titles of this book: Must the universe have a cause? Could the universe have an explanation? Are we the outcome of chance or design? These are very general questions, requiring us to examine the concepts they employ: cause, explanation, chance. What do these words mean? In what sort of cases are they applicable? Are there good arguments to the effect that everything must have a cause, or an explanation? Does it make sense to talk of the universe as a whole being the outcome of chance? This is the stuff of metaphysical enquiry. 'Metaphysics is the finding of bad reasons for what we believe on instinct.' F.H. Bradley's satirical comment is not, I hope, entirely accurate. The metaphysician tries, at least, to look for good reasons rather than bad, and the conclusions of metaphysical arguments are more often surprising than instinctive.

The questions that are addressed in the following pages are both metaphysical questions and religious ones. Consider one of the deepest problems in philosophy: why is there something rather than nothing? We, living things, the planet we inhabit, the entire cosmos – all these might not have existed. There might have been absolutely nothing at all. As it is sometimes put, all existence is contingent. For some, this is an appalling thought, as the idea that existence is in some sense a random occurrence, and not a necessary one, seems to rob it of meaning. Reflections of this sort are the life-blood of religion, because religion offers to bring us back from the abyss. No, it tells us, your life is not a purely random event, it has a meaning, a purpose. To religion we may turn to find answers to deep metaphysical questions.

But *should* we turn to religion for such answers? There are two quite different conceptions of religion, one that I shall call 'metaphysical', and the other 'non-metaphysical'. Let us begin with the question, what is religion? Or, since there are a number of quite distinct religions, perhaps our question should be: what is it that religions have in common? Not, certainly, the idea that there is a transcendent being who created and ordered the universe and to whom we are ultimately answerable. This is, it is true, the central theme of Christianity, Judaism and Islam. Such religions are 'theistic' – 'theism', as we said above, being simply the doctrine, denied by *a*theism, that God exists. Some religions, however, are *non*-theistic. Buddhism, for example, does not teach the existence of a deity. So it is important to bear in mind that theism is simply one form of religion.

I suggest that a religion, whether theistic or not, consists of two components. The first is a practical component, which is a way of life, including not only ritualistic behaviour specific to the religion in question, but also a view about what it is best for one to do, and how to achieve self-fulfilment. This practical component is based on a second component, which is a picture of the world. Now, on the metaphysical conception of religion, this picture is a metaphysical outlook, a certain theory about reality which is not directly revealed by ordinary, everyday experience. This outlook might contain the idea of a creator, or it might be a view about what happens to us after death. It cannot be refuted by appeal to what appears to be the case, because it is a theory about what underlies those appearances. A religion, then, on this account, is a way of life based on a metaphysical conception of the world. Religious doctrine contains, therefore, what are essentially explanatory hypotheses.

As I have presented it, this is at best rather a sketchy account, and it does not exclude beliefs which we would hesitate to describe as religious. Consider fatalism, the view that, since everything is determined, we have no genuine choices, and that there is therefore no point in trying to affect the outcome of things. Is this a religious outlook or not? Perhaps we should include, in our characterisation of religion, the condition that a religious outlook is essentially positive, in that it emphasises our worth as agents. But was Calvinism positive in this respect? I do not wish to get involved in such arguments here, but only to emphasise that, on one view, religion is, in part, metaphysics.

In contrast to this view is the *non*-metaphysical conception of religion. Over the last few decades, a number of leading figures in the Anglican Church have argued for a shift in the way we think of talk 'about' God. We should, they contend, give up a literal picture of God as a being like us, only infinitely greater, and think instead of religious language as symbolic, figurative, metaphorical. Not surprisingly, those who have argued in this way, such as Bishop John Robinson in the 1960s and, more recently, Don Cupitt, have been branded 'atheist priests'. In a sense, the label is not entirely inappropriate, for they are denying (and, in Cupitt's case, in the most explicit terms) a God who exists entirely independently of our thoughts about him. But, and here the distinction between religion and theism is crucial, these 'radical theologians' are not, by virtue of such a denial, irreligious. They are not rejecting Christianity as a set of practices, images and ideals. On the contrary, they see it as continuing to have a fundamental role in our spiritual lives. What Cupitt and others have urged is that Christianity should abandon its traditional metaphysical basis, and reject the notion of a 'metaphysical God', i.e. a creator who exists independently of us. On this view, religious statements are not explanatory hypotheses about such things as why the world exists. They serve, rather, to provide a fictional picture which guides us in our moral lives.

Now, whether we adopt the metaphysical or the non-metaphysical stance, philosophical argument is relevant, for, if religious statements are intended as true descriptions of the world, we need to ask whether they truly explain anything, and what their implications are. And if they are not intended as true descriptions, we need to ask how they can have spiritual and moral significance.

I now turn to the structure and argument of this book. Running throughout is one central concern: can atheism be rationally justified? We cannot provide a full assessment of atheism, however, without engaging with arguments in favour of theism. Here are some of the most important of those arguments:

(a) The universe cannot have come into existence from nothing: it must have had an ultimate cause, namely God.
(b) The existence of God explains what would otherwise be entirely mysterious, namely, why the laws of nature are such as to have permitted the emergence of intelligent life.
(c) Only by supposing that there is a God can we make sense of the idea that there are objective moral values, that there is a difference between what is right and what is wrong quite independent of any social convention.
(d) Unless there is a God who offers the chance of eternal life, death is the end of everything for us, all things are merely transient, and the inexorable passage of time makes every project we undertake ultimately futile.

These arguments have a very powerful intuitive appeal, and the atheist will need to address them. Accordingly, in Chapter 1, I begin with a more refined version of argument (a), namely the *cosmological argument*. Two versions of this are explored. The first argues that the universe must have had a cause, because it had a beginning, and nothing can come into existence without a cause. The second argues that the universe must have a cause, or at least an explanation of its existence, because it might not have existed. This suggests that something whose existence is necessary – i.e. it is impossible for it *not* to exist – would not need an explanation for, or a cause of, its existence. That God necessarily exists is the conclusion of another famous proof of theism, the *ontological argument*. This is discussed in

Chapter 2. Both the cosmological and ontological arguments fail, I argue. But we are still left with the feeling that the absence of a causal explanation for the universe is unsatisfactory. That feeling is mis-placed, however, as I argue in Chapter 3. Nothing could count as a *causal* explanation of the existence of the universe. This nevertheless leaves the door open for some alternative explanation, one in terms of purpose. This is the theme of Chapter 4, which engages with argument (b) above. Again, a more precise statement of this can be found in a third traditional proof of God's existence, the *teleological argument*. Most time is spent on a relatively modern version of this argument, which turns on the idea that, unless there were a God who intended that there should be life, the probability of the laws of nature being compatible with life (at least, as we know it) would have been very small. I argue that this involves a misuse of the notion of probability, just as the cosmological argument involves a misuse of the concept of causation.

In Part I of the book, then, the case for atheism consists largely of a critique of some traditional arguments for God. One idea explored in these chapters is that, even if the traditional arguments fail, the theist can still urge that theism provides an explanation when atheism does not. Each of the arguments for God can be presented as an attempt to demonstrate that theism provides important explanations of certain things. The case against them is that such 'theistic explanation' is very limited. But even a limited explanation, it might be said, is better than no explanation at all. Argument (b) remains a mystery for the atheist. Or does it? Can the atheist explain why the laws of nature were such as to permit life? This is addressed in Chapter 5, which concludes Part I. The *moral explanation* of the laws of nature is introduced: the laws of nature were such as to permit the emergence of life in order to allow the evolution of moral agents. The moral explanation runs into difficulties, however, once we realise the dependence of purposive explanation on underlying causal relations. Given this, we cannot make sense of moral explanation outside theism. This particular atheist strategy, then, fails.

In Part II, the atheist goes on the offensive, and puts forward two moral arguments against the existence of God. The first of these turns argument (c) on its head, and faces the theist with the following dilemma, presented in Chapter 6: either moral values are quite independent of God, or the assertion that God is good and wills us to do what is good is virtually meaningless. I consider ways in which the theist can avoid this dilemma. In Chapter 7, the most famous argument for atheism, *the problem of evil*, is introduced. How can the existence of a loving and all-powerful God be reconciled with the atrocious suffering of many of his creatures? An attractive solution to the problem is that suffering is the inevitable outcome of God's gift to human beings of genuine freedom of will. This solution is criticised in some detail.

If we are convinced by the arguments against theism, we are faced with a choice between two kinds of atheism. The first rejects all talk of God. The second takes a more liberal stance, and makes room for a reinterpretation of talk about God as not being descriptive.

Part III begins with the issue of whether traditionally theist religions can survive rejection of the literal truth of theism. The difficulty is to explain how talk about God, when reinterpreted as non-fact-stating, can continue to have an emotional effect on us. I set out this 'non-realist' approach to theistic religion in Chapter 8, drawing on the debate between realists and non-realists in the philosophy of science. In order to explain how religious language and practice can exert an emotional effect, even when not taken to be literally true, I explore an analogy with our emotional engagement with fiction. In Chapter 9, an intriguing argument of Rudolf Carnap's is discussed, to the effect that questions about what exists in reality are somehow improper, and should be abandoned. Finally, in Chapter 10, we turn to the issue of death. To echo point (d) above, if we reject, not only theism, but any religious outlook in which there is the possibility of life after death, does the transience of existence not rob it of real value? I suggest in this last chapter that our dismay at the thought of death is closely bound up with a particular metaphysical view of time, in particular of time's passage. A different conception of time is put forward which, it is suggested, makes death a less awful prospect.

Metaphysics is not a collection of esoteric aphorisms far removed from human affairs. It concerns fundamental questions about the world and our place in it, as I hope the following pages will show.

# Part I

# The limits of theistic explanation

# 1 Must the universe have a cause?

Nothing will come of nothing.

William Shakespeare, *King Lear*

## THE MYSTERIES OF EXISTENCE

Why does the universe exist? Why do living things exist? Why do intelligent beings capable of suffering exist? These are among the most fundamental questions we can ask, and one of the most appealing reasons to believe in the existence of a benevolent creator is that it seems to answer them, whereas atheism seems unable to do so.

For the atheist, the universe is all that there is. There is nothing outside it. Consequently, there is nothing to point to as a cause of the universe's existence. So why there is something, rather than nothing, remains a mystery. Similarly, the evolution of life, from the atheist's perspective, serves no wider purpose. Life simply exists, it seems, for no other reason than its own perpetuation through reproduction. And the fact that the constitution of the universe should happen to have been such as to permit the evolution of life, and that exactly the right conditions for the evolution of life were realised, is similarly mysterious. Once we suppose there to be a creator, however, who has intentions and the limitless power to act on those intentions, these mysteries disappear.

Or do they? *Does* theism provide answers to the mysteries of existence? Is the atheist unable to produce rival, and equally satisfying, answers? Are the mysteries themselves genuine mysteries at all, or merely symptoms of fundamental intellectual confusion? Whether theism does indeed provide answers where atheism does not is the main theme of the first part of this book. We shall begin by looking at one influential and compelling argument for a creator of the universe which exploits our puzzlement over the existence and nature of that universe: the cosmological argument.

## A FIRST CAUSE?

There are, in fact, a number of cosmological arguments. What they have in common is an observation about some very general feature of the universe, and the assertion that something must be the ultimate cause, or at least the ultimate explanation, of that feature. The arguments we shall examine conclude that the existence of the universe itself must have a cause. This cause cannot be part of the universe itself, for otherwise there would be something which caused itself to exist, and this, we intuitively think, is impossible. For example, suppose we believe, on the authority of a number of physicists, that the universe originated in the so-called 'Big Bang': an explosion from an almost infinitesimally small region of enormous density. We might say that everything that occurred *after* the Big Bang was caused by the Big Bang. But since the Big Bang is part of the universe's history, we must include the Big Bang as part of what we are referring to by 'the universe'. It would then be quite mistaken to say that 'The Big Bang was the cause of the universe', for this would mean 'The Big Bang was the cause of the Big Bang and everything that came afterwards'. So, if the universe as a whole has a cause, this cause is not the Big Bang.

In this chapter we shall look at three versions of the cosmological argument. The first I shall call the *basic* cosmological argument, because the other two are modifications of it. It goes as follows:

*The basic cosmological argument*

1   Anything that exists has a cause of its existence.
2   Nothing can be the cause of its own existence.
3   The universe exists.

*Therefore:* The universe has a cause of its existence which lies outside the universe.

Although no-one has defended a cosmological argument of precisely this form, it provides a useful stepping-stone to the other, more sophisticated, versions. Before discussing it, we might note that the view that the cause of the universe's existence should be an intelligent, benevolent creator who has an interest in his creation clearly requires more than this very brief argument. An argument for God, as he is conceived of by the theist, must surely involve a series of interconnected arguments, each contributing some further aspect to our understanding of God. Nevertheless, being persuaded by an argument for a cause of the universe is to take a large step towards theism.

Most proponents of cosmological arguments insist that the universe has not merely a cause but a *first* cause: something which is not caused by anything else. Now the first two premises of the basic argument,

1 Anything that exists has a cause of its existence.
2 Nothing can be the cause of its own existence.

are actually incompatible with the existence of a first cause. For if *everything* has a cause outside itself, then we are inevitably led to an infinite regression of causes: A was caused by B, which was caused by C, which was caused ... etc. So, if we want to allow the possibility of a first cause, we must modify either (1) or (2). We could restrict either or both of them just to the parts of the universe, being careful, however, to include the universe itself as something which has a cause. Premise (1) could thus become:

Anything which exists *and is not outside the universe* has a cause of its existence.

We are, presumably, safe in assuming that the universe itself is not outside the universe. The problem with this amendment of the first premise, however, is that it seems rather arbitrary. We need to specify *what* it is about the universe which requires both it and anything within it to have a cause. This takes us to the two influential variants of the basic argument.

## THE TEMPORAL AND MODAL COSMOLOGICAL ARGUMENTS

How else, then, may we amend the first premise, that everything has a cause? It is certainly true that everything that we can directly observe seems to have a cause of its existence. At least, this is true of clouds, houses, mountains, rivers, and so on. But what is also true is that these things all *began* to exist at a certain time, and the fact that they began to exist when they did, and not earlier or later, calls for causal explanation. Now, arguably, it is *only* those things which began to exist at a certain time whose existence calls for causal explanation. If something began to exist at some time, we can point to a time before it existed and say that that was when the cause of the thing's existence occurred. But if something has always existed, then we cannot point to a time before it existed. This suggests that things which have always existed have no cause. If this is so, then the proponent of the cosmological argument should offer a more restricted first premise:

1a Everything that begins to exist has a cause of its existence.

But what of the universe? Did it begin to exist, or has it always existed?

According to the Big Bang theory, the universe *did* have a beginning. If we are confident of this, then we can offer a more restricted form of the argument, which I shall call the *temporal* cosmological argument, as follows:

### The temporal cosmological argument

1a   Everything that begins to exist has a cause of its existence.
2    Nothing can be the cause of its own existence.
3a   The universe began to exist.

*Therefore:* The universe has a cause of its existence which lies outside the universe.

So, to the question 'What is it about the universe which requires it to have a cause?', the proponent of the temporal argument can answer: the fact that the universe has a beginning. What is special about the first cause is that it has no beginning, and that is why it does not require a cause. So a regress of causes may be avoided.

Can we be confident about premise (3a), however? Suppose that the Big Bang theory is false – not an unreasonable supposition since, after all, cosmological theories are highly controversial, and even if there were universal agreement among physicists on this question – which is not the case – such agreement would not make the theory true. For all we know, the universe may not have had a beginning. This suggests two possibilities: (i) The universe extends infinitely far into the past; (ii) The universe is temporally closed: i.e., it is finite yet has neither a beginning nor an end. The first of these is perhaps easier to contemplate than the second, though both make considerable demands on our imagination. On the first view, we can represent the history of the universe as a series of events laid out along a line and which has no first member. Let us call this the 'infinite past' model.

$$\ldots S_{t-4} \Rightarrow S_{t-3} \Rightarrow S_{t-2} \Rightarrow S_{t-1} \Rightarrow S_t$$

*Figure 1.1* The infinite past model

'$S_t$' denotes all the events occurring in the universe at a particular time, $t$. '$S_{t-1}$' denotes all the events occurring at an earlier time, $t-1$, etc. Some, perhaps all, of the events occurring at $t$ will be caused by events occurring at $t-1$. In this sense, every member of the series has an antecedent cause. Since the series has no first member, no member is without a cause. On the second view, in contrast, we should represent the history of the universe as a series of events laid out around a circle. Let us call this the 'closed time' model.

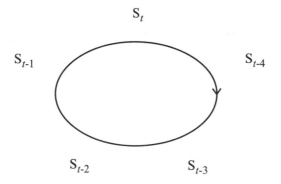

*Figure 1.2* The closed time model

Here, again, there is no first member of the series: every event is preceded by some other event. But, unlike the infinite past model, the closed time model represents the history of the universe as only finitely extended: the past does not stretch indefinitely far back. However, although the past is only finite, it does not have a beginning, for all the events which occur before, e.g. $S_t$, also occur *after* $S_t$. A simple analogy for this view of the universe is provided by the surface of the earth: if you set out from some point on the equator, remain on the equator, and do not go through the same place more than once, your journey will only be finitely long; not because you will eventually reach a barrier through which you cannot pass, but because you will end up at your starting point.

It is tempting to be misled by this analogy with the earth's surface and suppose that the situation represented by Fig. 1.2 is that of history repeating itself. Just as we can go round and round the earth's surface, so we may imagine that, having come back to $S_t$, the universe will go round again and repeat the past sequence of events in the same order. But the situation represented by Fig. 1.2 is not that of history repeating itself. The events occur once and once only, but no event is the first. For example, take the event of my birth. The closed time model entails, not that I will be born again, but (and this will no doubt seem rather puzzling) that my birth is both in the relatively recent past *and* in the future – though the very distant future, if the circle is a large one.

Both on the infinite past model and on the closed time model, the universe does not have a beginning. The temporal cosmological argument does not therefore apply in these cases, because premise (3a), that the universe began to exist, would be false. Precisely because the temporal version of the argument seems to give hostages to empirical fortune in this way, some defenders of the cosmological argument might prefer not to restrict the first premise just to things which have a beginning. And perhaps they would be right not to do so, for, if *only* things which have a beginning have a cause for their existence, then the discovery of conclusive evidence that the universe did not have a beginning would be a serious threat to belief in a creator.

To recapitulate the discussion so far, the cosmological argument concludes that there is a cause of the universe (or some feature of the universe), namely God. The more general version of the argument starts from the premise that everything that exists has a cause. It was then suggested that only things that *begin* to exist need to be explained in causal terms, and thus that the universe only has a cause if it has a beginning. Can this assumption be questioned? Is it possible that, even if the universe is as portrayed in Fig. 1.1 or Fig. 1.2, it may still have a cause? Here is a reason for thinking so. Although it is true, both on the infinite past model and on the closed time model, that each event in the history of the universe has a cause, we do not thereby have a causal explanation of the existence of *the universe as a whole*. We can answer the question, 'Why did this or that particular event occur when it did?' But we cannot answer the question, 'Why does the universe exist at all?' This question remains, whichever view of the universe we adopt. So we should leave the door open for a causal explanation of both an infinite past world and a closed time world.

But, then, what exactly is it, if not the fact that it has a beginning, that makes the existence of the universe mysterious, and that motivates us to look for a cause? One answer is that the existence of a universe is a purely *contingent* matter. That is, although there is in fact a universe, things might have been otherwise: there might have been no universe at all. It is not impossible for there to have been absolutely nothing. And this is a feature of things which have causes, that their existence is a purely contingent matter. This reflection suggests another way of restricting the first premise of the basic argument, providing us with a third version, which I shall call the *modal* cosmological argument. (In this context, the word 'modal' refers to matters of necessity and possibility, ideas which we will look at more closely in the next chapter.) It goes as follows:

*The modal cosmological argument*

1b  Everything whose existence is contingent has a cause of its existence.
2   Nothing can be the cause of its own existence.
3b  The existence of the universe is contingent.

*Therefore:* The universe has a cause of its existence which lies
outside the universe.

This, or something like it, is sometimes called 'the argument from
contingency'. Like the temporal argument, the modal argument allows
for the existence of a first cause. In this case, however, the first cause
would have to be something whose existence was not contingent, but
necessary. That is, it would have been impossible for it not to exist. Only
so could it lack a cause.

The plausibility of (3b), unlike that of (3a), does not depend in any
way upon the outcome of scientific investigation. Because of this, the
modal cosmological argument may seem more defensible than the
temporal version. However, as we shall see in Chapter 3, there are
problems with the notion of a necessary being as a cause of the
universe.

It seems, then, as if there are ways to avoid a regress of causes. Let us
now look at the first premises of the temporal and modal cosmological
arguments.


## PROBLEMS WITH THE FIRST PREMISE

'Everything that begins to exist has a cause of its existence.' How secure is
this premise? A toadstool appears overnight in my garden. Seeing it the
next morning, I am led to wonder both why it appeared at all and why it
appeared last night and not sooner. With my elementary grasp of
biology, I reason that there must have been spores in the soil. I reason
further that conditions favoured the appearance of toadstools last night:
there was sufficient moisture, there had been no hard frost, and any
number of other important factors were present. Were I to study the
spores in detail I should no doubt discover some internal physiological
mechanism which, in conjunction with external conditions, was responsible for the appearance of the toadstool at just that time. To generalise:
things come into existence because of the conditions that obtained just
prior to their appearance.

Some will object that this generalisation is simply unjustified, for
modern physics has discovered both that there are some phenomena at
the sub-atomic level which occur quite randomly, and that, at or near
the time of the Big Bang, the laws of physics break down, and so what
emerges from the Big Bang is unpredictable. Therefore, the suggestion
goes, there are things which begin to exist, and whose existence is purely
contingent, which yet are uncaused. I think we should be very cautious
about these grounds for rejecting the first premise. Physics itself is in a

state of rapid development, and whatever theories are on offer at a particular time are not only the subject of controversies among physicists but are also liable to be replaced at some later date. We should, in any case, be wary of the move from 'unpredictable' to 'uncaused'. We may simply be unable to discern, for reasons to do with the laws themselves, what laws are operating both at the sub-atomic level and at the Big Bang. So, rather than trying to attack directly the premise that everything that begins to exist has a cause, let us instead ask what authority it has. Is it simply a deeply held conviction? A guess? Or something more than that?

Let us look at three suggestions, each of them attempting to explain how the premise could count as something we *know* to be true. The first suggestion is that we know it to be true *a priori*, and this is because it is *analytically* true. The second suggestion is that we know it to be true *a priori*, but it is not analytically true. The third suggestion is that we do not know it to be true *a priori*, but rather we infer it inductively from our observations. I shall assume that these three answers exhaust the possible explanations of how the premise could count as a piece of knowledge. What do they mean?

Let us begin with the first suggestion. We know something to be true *a priori* if we can verify it without having to rely directly on observation or experience. For example, we know that twelve plus six equals eighteen without having to observe a group of twelve objects being added to a group of six objects and then counting the resulting group. Provided that we understand the number system, we can work out such a simple sum in our heads. Of course, in order to gain an understanding of the number system, we needed to have the requisite experiences, perhaps by manipulating counters, but once having acquired this understanding, we no longer need to appeal to experience in order to perform mathematical calculations. Now we know some propositions to be true *a priori* because they are also *analytically* true. So what is it for something to be analytically true? There is some disagreement amongst philosophers on this. On one account, analytic truths are those which are true by virtue of the meanings of the words. On another, analytic truths are those whose negations are self-contradictory. (The negation of a sentence is simply the result of putting 'It is not the case that' before that sentence.) An example of a sentence which both accounts would judge to be analytic is 'Anaesthetics reduce sensitivity to pain.' Suppose I sincerely asserted that I had just invented an anaesthetic that heightened people's sensitivity to pain. I could surely not have grasped the meaning of the term 'anaesthetic'. You would know that my assertion was false because 'anaesthetic' *means* something which reduces one's sensitivity to pain. You do not need to step into my laboratory to see whether my assertion is true or not. The statement that 'I have invented an anaesthetic which heightens people's sensitivity to pain' implies that there is an anaesthetic which does *not* reduce sensitivity to pain, and this is self-contradictory.

For a large number of examples, the two accounts of analyticity agree on whether a proposition should be classified as analytic or not. Either will do for our purposes, but for simplicity I shall use 'analytic' to mean 'has a self-contradictory negation'.

So, to return to our premise, can it plausibly be regarded as analytically true? No. Someone who sincerely asserted that there were, or might be, some things which began to exist and yet were not caused would not obviously be contradicting themselves. It is true that we might be highly puzzled by the thought of something's coming into existence without a cause, since there would apparently be no explanation of why it came into existence when it did, nor indeed of why it came into existence at all. But such puzzlement is not the same as discovering a contradiction in the idea, and may arise simply because a thing without a cause is contrary to our experience.

As we said above, if something is analytically true, then we can know it to be true *a priori*. However, there may be some things that we know *a priori* but which cannot be captured by either of our definitions of 'analytic'. Kant thought that geometrical propositions were of this kind (though his characterisation of the analytic does not coincide precisely with either of our two definitions), and he labelled them 'synthetic *a priori*' truths. 'Synthetic' here simply means 'non-analytic'. One possible example of a synthetic *a priori* truth is 'Nothing is both red all over and green all over'. We do not need to verify this by appeal to experience, so we know it to be true *a priori*. But it is far from clear that its truth is guaranteed simply by the meaning of the words, or that 'Something is both red all over and green all over' is self-contradictory. In other words, it appears to be synthetic. Now if there are such things as synthetic *a priori* truths, then the possibility remains that the first premise is one such truth. This takes us to our second suggestion. Here it might be objected that we can at least conceive of the idea of something's not having a cause, whereas we cannot conceive of the falsity of an *a priori* truth. (Try conceiving of something's being red all over and green all over at the same time.) This will not convince defenders of the cosmological argument, however. We may conceive of an event without conceiving of its cause, they will say, but this is not to conceive of an event which has no cause. There is, however, another objection to this suggestion, which I shall present later.

What, finally, of the third suggestion? This was that we know that things that begin to exist have causes because we *inductively infer* it from observation. Here is an example of a – not very safe – inductive inference. I observe that the 12.20 train from Oxenholme to Windermere has been late four days running, and infer from this that this service is always late. Another example of such an inference is the inference from the fact that the British Conservative Party has won the last four general elections that it will win the next one. Yet another is the inference from the observation that a crow is black to the conclusion that all crows are black. Clearly, some inductive inferences are safer than others, but they all have a common form, which we can characterise as follows: an inductive inference is one which moves from a premise about some members of a certain class to a conclusion either about some of the other members of that class or about all the members of that class. The third suggestion, then, is that we infer from our observation of things and their causes, that everything that begins to exist has a cause.

Now, if the first premise is to support the conclusion of the cosmological argument, 'everything' must include the universe itself. So, if the third suggestion is correct, our experience justifies us in positing a cause for the universe. But the causes which we have experience of take place in time and space, and this is not an accidental connection. We suppose things to have causes because we want to explain why those things came into existence *at the times and places they did*. We therefore look for the causes of those things in the conditions which obtained just before, and in the vicinity of, the thing in question. Conditions which obtained elsewhere or at other times cannot provide the relevant explanation. Causation, then, is a *temporal* concept. (It is perhaps also a spatial concept, but I do not want to insist on that here.) It is this aspect of causation which threatens the inference from what we experience to a conclusion about everything which begins to exist.

Suppose the universe has a beginning in time, as the temporal cosmological argument requires. Three possibilities present themselves. The first is that time itself has a beginning, one which coincides with the beginning of the universe. The second is that there is a finite period of time before the beginning of the universe. The third is that there is an infinite period of time before the beginning of the universe. If the first of these possibilities obtains, then the universe cannot have a cause, at least not in the ordinary sense, for in the ordinary sense the cause of the existence of a thing is something which occurs just before the thing begins to exist. But, if the beginning of time coincides with the beginning of the universe, then nothing could have occurred before the universe started to exist. If the second of the possibilities obtains, if it is true that everything that begins to exist has a cause, then the universe has a cause. But, since time itself has a beginning, it too must have a cause. But, by definition, nothing can occur before time itself. Time cannot have a cause for its existence, and so it provides a counter-example to the premise that everything that begins to exist has a cause. If the third possibility obtains, then, again, the universe can have a cause, but it would simply be the last member of an infinite chain of causes:

The beginning of the universe

⇑

$$... S_{t-4} \Rightarrow S_{t-3} \Rightarrow S_{t-2} \Rightarrow S_{t-1} \Rightarrow S_t$$

*Figure 1.3* The beginning of the universe on the infinite past model

Why is this? Why could the cause of the universe not be something like an eternal, immutable God, who needs no cause for his existence? Well, the mere existence of God, or of any other object, could not causally explain why the universe came into existence. It must be something *about* God which does the explaining, such as his willing the universe to exist. But has he, for all time, willed the universe to exist? Why, then, did it not come into existence sooner? If there is a cause of the universe's coming into existence at precisely the moment it did, then it is something which obtained just before that event. We are then led to ask why that cause obtained when it did, and so, by similar reasoning, we are led back to the regress of causes which the temporal argument was supposed to avoid. So either the first premise is false, because there *is* something which begins to exist yet has no cause, and so cannot be either a piece of *a priori* knowledge or the result of a sound inductive inference, or there is no *first* cause.

So far in this section, we have concentrated entirely on the first premise of the temporal cosmological argument. What of the first premise of the modal argument, that everything whose existence is contingent has a cause of its existence? This is not obviously something we know *a priori*, nor is it obviously something we infer from experience, but whatever the supposed basis of its authority, it faces the objection we have just been discussing: causation is essentially a temporal concept. So, if the universe is supposed to have a beginning, the problems we encountered above will still occur. The difference between the modal and temporal arguments is that the modal argument allows for the possibility of the universe's not having a beginning. But if it does not have a beginning, then it cannot have a cause in the ordinary sense, for nothing could then have occurred *before* the universe existed.

There is a further problem for the modal argument. According to the first premise, everything whose existence is contingent, i.e. everything which might not have existed, has a cause. But, arguably, time itself might not have existed: it too exists only contingently. So the first premise of the modal argument directs us to the conclusion that time itself has a cause. But since, as we noted above, nothing can occur before time itself, time cannot be said to have a cause.

We can conclude that, if the idea that the universe has a cause of its existence is to be defended, it must be on a very different understanding of 'cause' than the one with which we ordinarily operate. But, to justify the name, the 'cause' of the universe must at least play something like the role which ordinary causes play in our view of things. It must at least provide an explanation of why the universe exists. Whether such an explanation is possible is the subject of Chapter 3.

In this chapter, we have focused on the notion of causation. But the modal cosmological argument also introduces another important concept, that of necessity. It is now time to look at this notion.

### SUMMARY

An ancient and influential argument for the existence of a creator is the cosmological argument. We examined three versions, all of which exploit the notion of causality. The first, the basic argument, begins with the premise that everything that exists has a cause. The problem with this argument is that it implies an infinite regress of causes, whereas God is supposed to be a *first* cause: something not caused by anything else. The difficulty can be overcome, however, if we restrict the first premise in some way. This led us to two other versions of the argument. The second version, the temporal argument, begins with the premise that everything which *begins* to exist has a cause. This argument only establishes that the universe has a cause if it can be established that the universe has a beginning, and there is some doubt as to whether this could be established. This difficulty is avoided by the third version, the modal cosmological argument, which begins with the premise that everything whose existence is merely contingent, i.e. which might not have existed, has a cause.

The problem with both the temporal and the modal arguments is that they necessarily represent the first cause as being something utterly unlike ordinary causes. Our ordinary notion of causation is bound up intimately with the notion of time. Causes take place at particular moments of time, and before their effects. A first cause, however, would have a completely different relationship to time. So diffcrent, in fact, that we havc to admit that the universe cannot be said to have a cause in the ordinary sense of the word.

## FURTHER READING

For an introductory discussion of cosmological arguments, see Chapter 5 of Brian Davies, *An Introduction to the Philosophy of Religion*, 2nd Edition, Oxford: Oxford University Press, 1993.

The classic statement of a number of cosmological arguments is the 'five ways' of St Thomas Aquinas. See his *Summa Theologiae*, Part I, Question 2, Article 3. There are a number of editions of Aquinas's works: for example, Anton C. Pegis (ed.), *The Basic Writings of Saint Thomas Aquinas*, New York: Random House, 1945.

The temporal argument, under a different name, is discussed and defended at length in William Lane Craig's *The Kalam Cosmological Argument*, London: Macmillan, 1979. 'Kalam' is an Arabic word, and Craig traces the development of the argument in the writings of Arabic philosophers, to whom we owe both versions of the cosmological argument. Craig spends a large part of the book defending the second premise, that the universe had a beginning in time, which he believes can be established on *a priori* grounds. Parts of the book are reprinted in William Lane Craig and Quentin Smith, *Theism, Atheism and Big Bang Cosmology*, Oxford: Clarendon Press, 1993. Craig argues that Big Bang cosmology supports theism, whereas Smith argues that it supports atheism in so far as it implies that the universe could not have had a cause. Smith also criticises Craig's *a priori* arguments for the beginning of the universe.

See also Craig's *The Cosmological Argument from Plato to Leibniz*, London: Macmillan, 1980, from which one can get a clear idea of the enormous variety of cosmological arguments.

For a discussion of the relation between the cosmological argument and the topic of the next chapter, the notion of a necessary being, see Chapter 4 of William L. Rowe's *The Cosmological Argument*, Princeton: Princeton University Press, 1975.

The implications of the closed time model are explored in W.H. Newton-Smith's *The Structure of Time*, Routledge & Kegan Paul, 1980. For what now strikes me, for reasons given above, as a misguided attempt to reconcile the idea of a first cause with the closed time model, see Robin Le Poidevin, 'Creation in a Closed Universe *or*, Have Physicists Disproved the Existence of God?', *Religious Studies*, vol. 27 (1991), pp. 39–48.

A famous statement of the modal argument was given by Leibniz in his essay 'On the Ultimate Origination of Things', in *G.W. Leibniz, Philosophical Writings*, ed. G.H.R. Parkinson, London: J.M. Dent, 1973, pp. 136–44. It is given a sympathetic treatment in Richard Swinburne's *The Existence of God*, Oxford: Clarendon Press, 1979, Chapter 7.

# 2 Is God necessary?

How was the fool able to 'say in his heart' what he was unable to conceive?

St Anselm, *Proslogion*

## POSSIBLE WORLDS

According to the modal cosmological argument, that which makes us ask why the universe exists is the *contingency* of the universe: there might have been no universe, in the sense that its non-existence is a logical possibility. So, whatever provides the ultimate explanation, the first cause, must be non-contingent, or necessary. But these concepts of contingency, possibility and necessity (concepts concerning 'modality', as philosophers say) require some explication. I shall try to explicate them by introducing the useful, though controversial, idiom of 'possible worlds'. This idiom has become increasingly prevalent in philosophical writings over the last thirty years, though the idea seems to have originated in the writings of Leibniz.

We will begin by defining *the actual world*. The actual world includes everything that in fact exists: the sub-atomic particles, the earth, the solar system, the entire cosmos, space and time. We, of course, are part of the actual world, so we can call it '*this* world'. To give a complete description of the actual world – an impossible task – would be to describe everything that was, is and will be the case: that the earth has a moon, that the Roman Empire declined and fell, that France had a monarchy in the fourteenth century AD, that the Labour Party lost the 1992 British general election, and so on. Now this world could have been very different: there might have been four moons orbiting around the earth, the Roman Empire might never have declined and fallen, France might have been a republic in the fourteenth century, Neil Kinnock might have been Prime Minister in 1992. We can represent these possibilities as different *possible worlds*. (We can postpone for the moment the question of how precisely we are to conceive of these possible worlds. At present, we need think of them only as a useful device for representing talk about hypothetical situations.) Other possible worlds may be just as extensive as this one, but they are different in certain respects. In some cases, the differences are only trivial; in others, enormous. On the most liberal account, the only things that constrain the range of possible worlds are logic and mathematics: two inconsistent propositions can never both be true in any world; i.e., something cannot be both the case and not the case in the same possible world. For example, I cannot in one world be both six foot tall and not six foot tall at the same time. To say that pigs fly in some world is another way of saying that it is logically possible that pigs should fly. And to say that two plus two equals four in *all* worlds is another way of saying that it is logically necessary that two plus two equals four. We can define a sub-set of these worlds and talk, for example, of *physically possible* worlds: these are the worlds which are constrained by precisely the same laws of physics as obtain in this world.

The word 'world' has in this context, then, a quite different meaning from the one it has in ordinary speech, in which it is often used to mean the same as 'the earth'. Perhaps a little closer to the philosophical use is its meaning in the phrase 'She is in a world of her own'. The important point to bear in mind, however, is that, in what follows, 'world' means 'possible world', a way things could be.

Among the possible worlds are worlds where evolution developed up to the point of simple plants, but no further. In these worlds there is life, but no intelligence and no suffering. In other worlds, the universe remains completely barren: conditions in these worlds were never sufficiently stable to permit the existence of even unicellular organisms. In other, yet bleaker, worlds there is nothing at all: no object, no fields of force, just emptiness. So we can put one of the mysteries of existence in this form: why is this, the actual world, a world where there is a universe, and moreover a universe sufficiently stable to permit the emergence of life, rather than one in which there is complete emptiness?

Less dramatically, we sometimes reflect on how we could have been different. We might have had a different appearance, been somewhat shorter or taller, more or less intelligent, and we might have done quite different things, had we taken different decisions at certain crucial points in our lives. We often think: 'If only I had not done that ....' These possibilities are represented by the fact that we exist, not just in this world, but also in some other worlds where we have the properties that we might have had in this world. Although a writer of philosophy in this world, I am in some other world the discoverer of the laws of motion, in another the composer of *Così Fan Tutte*, in yet another the first person to have landed on the moon. Incidentally, in case you suppose these remarks to convict me of extreme egomania, I should point out that I am these things in other worlds, not because of any remarkable properties I possess in this world, but simply because such things are logically possible. In this sense, you too are the first person to have landed on the moon in some other world.

It may well be thought that we have simply introduced some gratuitous jargon in order to mystify perfectly straightforward questions – harmless enough, perhaps, but hardly explanatory. Well, as to its being harmless, some writers object to the whole notion of possible worlds, and we will, in fact, encounter reasons for being cautious in our use of the idiom later in this chapter. But even if we have only introduced another way of talking about possibility, rather than explaining its true nature, the idiom is still a very useful one, and it will be of particular value in helping us to understand one of the most intriguing and baffling arguments for the existence of God: the ontological argument.

## THE ONTOLOGICAL ARGUMENT

Like the cosmological argument, the ontological argument has been presented in a number of forms. What these have in common is this: they all argue that, if we simply understand what the concept of God involves, if we understand the definition of 'God', we must admit that God really exists. We shall look at the original version of the argument, presented by St Anselm, in this section. A more recent version of the argument, which makes explicit use of possible worlds, will be examined in the next section of this chapter.

In the *Proslogion*, Anselm defines God as 'that than which nothing greater can be conceived'. Now even the atheist must admit that he has the concept of such a thing, that God exists at least in our minds. What the atheist will insist, however, is that nothing in reality, existing independently of our minds, corresponds to this concept. But, in this, Anselm thinks that the atheist contradicts himself. If God existed *only* in our minds, as a concept, then we could conceive of a greater being, namely one who *really* existed. But then we would have thought of something greater than God, which, by definition, is impossible. So God does not merely exist in our minds, but in reality also.

We can set the argument out more systematically as follows:

*The ontological argument*

1   God exists either in our minds alone, or in reality also.

2   Something that exists in reality is greater than something which exists in the mind alone.
3   If God existed in our minds alone, then we could think of something greater, namely something which really exists.
4   We cannot, however, conceive of anything greater than God.

*Therefore:* God does not exist in the mind alone, but in reality also.

If this argument works, we can draw a much stronger conclusion than the one that God actually exists. What Anselm has tried to show is that, in denying the existence of God, the atheist ('the fool') contradicts himself, for something cannot both be 'that than which nothing greater can be conceived', and not exist. But since God is by definition that than which nothing greater can be conceived, it is *analytically true* (see Chapter 1, pages 10–11) that he exists. And, since all analytic truths are also necessary – they obtain in all possible worlds – it is necessarily true that God exists. That is, it is not possible for him not to exist. Now this is an interesting result, because it shows how the ontological argument could be used to support the modal cosmological argument. Because the universe is merely contingent, it requires (according to the modal cosmological argument) a cause. Now either this cause is itself caused, or it is something which exists necessarily, and so requires no cause. Now, there are difficulties with the notion of a cause of the universe, but we may still feel that there should be some ultimate *explanation* of why the universe exists, one which does not invite further explanation. If we can show, as the ontological argument tries to show, that there is a God who exists necessarily, we have, it seems, found the first cause postulated by the cosmological argument. A necessary being does not call for explanation. The two arguments thus fit together rather neatly: the ontological argument proves the existence of a necessary God, and the cosmological argument shows how the idea can be applied. But does the ontological argument work?

That something is wrong with the argument is indicated by the fact that, if it were successful, it could be used to prove the existence of a variety of things other than God. For example, I have an idea of 'that than which nothing *nastier* can be conceived'. Following Anselm's reasoning, surely a really existing nasty thing is nastier than a nasty thing which merely exists in my mind. So that than which *nothing* nastier can be conceived must surely really exist. Well, perhaps it does, and this only goes to show that there must be a Devil. But we can produce any number of parodies of the original argument. Consider the *noisiest* thing conceivable: it must exist, if Anselm is right, for otherwise it would be completely silent! We could people the world with all kinds of implausible entities in this way. Surely we cannot really have a licence to do this? (A similar objection was put by a contemporary of Anselm's named Gaunilo, who pointed out that we could similarly 'prove' the existence of the most perfect island.) This does not tell us, of course, what is wrong with the argument. It only encourages the suspicion that something is wrong. To show that the ontological argument is on safer ground than these parodies of it, Anselm must show that there is something special about greatness.

So let us begin by looking at the notion of greatness, which clearly plays a crucial role in the argument. What exactly is it to say that something is greater than something else? If we think of the properties traditionally ascribed to God, something could be said to be greater than something else if it is more powerful (can do a greater number of things, or do them more effectively), more knowledgeable, and morally superior. But, having understood this, it is far from clear how we are to apply it to the objects mentioned in premises (2) and (3) of the ontological argument. In what sense is it true that something which exists in reality is greater than something which exists only in the mind?

We need to be more clear, before we can answer this, about what it is to exist only in the mind. If something is in my mind, I have an idea of it. An idea is a representation, rather as a portrait is a painted representation of a person. (We should not be carried away by this analogy too far, however: I do not mean to suggest that an idea just *is* a mental picture.) The idea represents, or at least is supposed to represent, an object, and further represents it as having certain features. Now it may be that there is no object in the world which corresponds to that representation, nothing that the representation is actually true of, just as what appears to be a portrait can be of a merely imaginary figure. So for something to exist merely in my mind is for me to have a representation of some kind to which nothing in the world corresponds. So, perhaps when Anselm says that a really existing God is greater than a God which exists merely in his mind, he is saying that God is greater than any representation of God, just as the person whose portrait is being painted is greater (i.e. knows more, can do more) than the portrait itself. This is certainly true, for a representation, such as a painting, is clearly incapable of having thoughts or performing actions. But this cannot be the contrast Anselm had in mind, for when he thought of God he certainly would not have represented God as some mental state of his, or, if you prefer, as a pattern of stimulation in his brain. He would have represented God as a person capable of knowledge and action. Further, if premises (2) and (3) are comparing a real God and a representation of God, then the argument does not imply the conclusion. That is, we can concede that a real God would be greater than any representation of him, without having to concede that there is in fact such a God. All they imply is that, when I think of God as existing, I am not thinking of some *representation* as existing. But we need no argument to establish that. So when Anselm talked of God existing in the mind, he cannot have been talking of the idea itself, at least not if 'idea' means representation, but of what the idea, the representation, was of. But now we have a problem because, if God exists only in the mind, as an idea, then there is nothing in the world to which the idea corresponds, so we cannot even begin to make a comparison between a really existing God and one which exists only in the mind, because the second of these is nothing at all.

To avoid this difficulty, we have to introduce the notion of an imaginary, or fictional object. This allows us to say that *all* ideas, or other representations, represent an object. Some represent a real object, one which exists in the world. Others represent a merely fictional object. Thus, my idea of Queen Elizabeth I represents a real object (although she no longer exists), but my idea of the White Witch of Narnia represents a merely fictional object. A fictional or imaginary object, unlike a real object, has all the properties it is represented as having. We can now rephrase Anselm's central contention as follows: a real God is greater than a merely fictional God. But, provided we bear in mind the distinction between a fictional object and a representation of a fictional object, we have no reason to accept this contention. The fictional God, of course, exists only in a fiction. But *in that fiction* he is just as powerful, knowledgeable and good as the God (if there is one) who exists in reality. For, as we said above, a fictional object has all the properties it is represented as having. Since we represent God as the greatest thing conceivable, the fictional object to which that representation corresponds (we are not, incidentally, ruling out that there is also a real object to which the representation corresponds) is necessarily the greatest being conceivable. But, if this is so, then it is simply false that a really existing God is greater than a merely fictional God. To summarise, then: premises (2) and (3) are either making an inappropriate comparison, between a real object and a representation of that object, in which case they are true but do not imply the conclusion of the argument, or they are false.

It may be helpful to restate the argument, and our objection to it, in different terms, ones which employ the notion of possible worlds. This is not, of course, how Anselm himself conceived of his argument, but I believe we are not unduly distorting his ideas by casting them in the idiom of worlds. The point of restating the argument in these terms is that it enables us to state our objection more simply, by avoiding (at least explicit) talk of representations and their objects.

Suppose, instead of saying 'God exists at least in our minds', or 'We have an idea of God', we say 'God exists at least in some possible world'. And instead of defining God as 'That than which nothing greater can be conceived', we define him as 'That which is greater than any other object in any possible world'. We can then run through Anselm's reasoning in the following form: either God exists only in other possible worlds, or he exists also in the actual world. If he merely existed in other worlds, we could think of a greater being, namely one who existed in this, the actual world. An actually existing being is greater than a merely possible being. But since God is by definition necessarily greater than everything else, he must exist in the actual world.

What is wrong with this argument? Suppose we are making a comparison, in terms of greatness, between two objects, A and B. Now if A and B exist in the same world, there is no difficulty, at least in principle. We simply determine which is the more powerful, etc. But the argument requires us to compare objects in different worlds: actual objects with merely possible objects. So, if A exists in one world, and B exists in another, we have to determine whether A is greater in the world in which A exists than B in the world in which B exists. Thus we could say that Zeus is greater than Charlie Chaplin – even though Charlie Chaplin actually existed whereas Zeus did not – if, in the worlds in which Zeus exists, he is more powerful, more knowledgeable, etc. than Chaplin is in the worlds in which *he* exists. Now we have defined God as 'That which is greater than any other object in any possible world', and what this means is that God is more powerful, more knowledgeable, etc. in the worlds in which he exists than any other object in the worlds in which that object exists. We now, however, have absolutely no reason to say that a God who exists in the actual world is greater than one which merely exists in some other possible world, for what this means is 'An actually existing God is greater in the worlds in which he exists than a merely possible God in the worlds in which he exists.' This is simply false. An actual God is omnipotent, omniscient and perfectly good in this world. A merely possible God is omnipotent, omniscient and perfectly good in other worlds. There is no difference, in terms of greatness, between them.

Of course, we could insist that it is greatness in the actual world which we are concerned with, and by 'God' we mean the greatest thing in this world. But then 'God' in this sense may turn out to be the President of the United States of America, and not an omnipotent, omniscient and perfectly good being at all.

The only way that we can make the argument work, in the sense of being valid and having true premises, is by building actual existence into the notion of greatness, so that existence, like power, is a 'great-making' property. It then irresistibly follows that the greatest thing possible must actually exist, but no atheist is going to accept a definition of God on *that* understanding of greatness.

## THE MODAL ONTOLOGICAL ARGUMENT

We suggested earlier that the cosmological argument, in its modal form, and the ontological argument go naturally together. According to the modal cosmological argument, all contingent things have a cause. If this is right, then any first – i.e. uncaused – cause, if there were one, would have to be non-contingent: it would have to exist as a matter of necessity. Now, if the ontological argument were sound, there would indeed be a being who necessarily existed, and who would therefore be able to fill the role of first cause and ultimate explanation of the universe. Unfortunately, the ontological argument examined in the previous section is not sound. But let us pursue further the idea that *if* there were a first cause, it would exist necessarily, in all possible worlds. There is a mathematical analogy here. Arithmetical statements such as 'two plus two equals four' are often used as the paradigmatic instances of necessary truths. That is, it is widely held that it is impossible for such statements to be false. Now, it is less widely held, but held nevertheless by a significant minority of philosophers, that the truth of arithmetical statements requires the reality of numbers. So, just as the statement 'Most Liberal Democrat supporters turned out to vote' requires the existence of people for its truth, 'two plus two equals four' requires, according to the theory, the existence of numbers. These numbers are not thought of as concrete entities which we can observe, like tables, but as abstract entities, existing outside space and time. But, though abstract, they are just as real as concrete objects. Now, if this theory is correct, and arithmetical statements are necessarily true, it would appear to follow that numbers necessarily exist: they exist in all worlds in which arithmetical statements are true, which is to say, all worlds. Here now is the analogy with God: even if we were uncertain as to whether the theory of the reality of numbers was true or not, we would concede that *if* numbers exist then, because they are required for the truth of arithmetical statements, they necessarily exist. That is, if they exist in the actual world, they exist in all worlds. Similarly, even if we are uncertain whether God exists or not, it remains true that *if* God exists in the actual world, he exists in all worlds.

Or so runs a plausible train of thought. It seems to be one which the atheist could accept for, after all, nothing so far has been said which implies that God does, in fact, exist in the actual world. All that has been said is that God, if he exists, is not a contingent being. But this means that he cannot be a merely possible object. For suppose God exists in some other world, though not in this one. He would, in that world, be a contingent being, by virtue of the fact that he exists only in some worlds, and not others. Since he cannot be merely contingent, he must exist either in all worlds, or in none. That is, either he necessarily exists, or it is impossible for him to exist. Therefore, if it is possible for God to exist, he necessarily exists. If he exists in any possible world, he exists in all worlds, and therefore in this, the actual world. Can we extend this train of thought any further? Well, it may be argued, it is clearly *possible* for God to exist for, after all, we cannot discern any contradiction in the idea of his existing. But, if it is possible for him to exist, and he cannot be a merely contingent object, then he necessarily exists. And if he necessarily exists, then he actually exists. We have now spelt out another version of the ontological argument, one which, like the argument presented in the previous section, deduces God's existence from the definition of 'God'. Because this second version explicitly makes use of the notions of necessity and possibility, we may call it the *modal* ontological argument. Here is the simplest way of presenting it:

*The modal ontological argument*

1  If it is possible for God to exist, then necessarily, God exists.
2  It is possible for God to exist.

*Therefore:* Necessarily, God exists.

Premise (1) follows from the principle that God cannot be a merely contingent being, and (2) from the fact that the statement 'God exists' is not self-contradictory. The assumption here is that necessary truths are *analytic* truths, and that necessary falsehoods, i.e. propositions which could not possibly be true, are *analytic* falsehoods, i.e. they are self-contradictions. Any proposition which is not an analytic falsehood is, according to this assumption, possibly true. So (2) is supposedly true because the statement 'God exists' is not analytically false. But this idea, that necessary truth/falsehood is the same thing as analytic truth/ falsehood, has dire consequences for the argument, for we can construct a modal argument for atheism which is the mirror-image of the ontological argument:

*The modal atheistic argument*

1   If it is possible for God to exist, then necessarily, God exists.
2a  It is possible that God does not exist.

*Therefore* (from 2a): It is not the case that necessarily, God exists.
*Therefore:* It is not possible for God to exist.

The argument for (2a) is that the idea of God's not existing is not self-contradictory, and that what is not self-contradictory is possibly true. The first conclusion follows from (2a), and we can represent the reasoning as follows: if God does not exist in some possible world, then clearly it cannot be the case that he exists in all worlds. The second conclusion follows from (1) and the first conclusion on the principle that the statements 'If *p* then *q*' and 'It is not the case that *q*' jointly entail the statement 'It is not the case that *p*'.

The first premise of both arguments is the same. We can take it as equivalent to the assertion that God is either necessary or impossible. The theist goes on to assert that, since it is obviously possible for God to exist, he must be necessary. The atheist, in contrast, asserts that, since it is obviously possible for God not to exist, he must be impossible. It is, perhaps, surprising that the two arguments come to such different conclusions, given that they have the same first premise, and that the second premise of one does not seem to conflict with the second premise of the other. In fact, (2) and (2a) do conflict, but *only on the assumption that the first premise is correct.* In other words, (1), (2) and (2a) cannot *all* be true together: they form an inconsistent set. But if all necessary truths are analytic, then both (2) and (2a) are true. Therefore, we must either reject the identification of necessary truth with analytic truth, or reject the first premise.

Let us take these moves a little more slowly. Suppose that all necessary truths are analytic. Then anything which is not analytic is not necessarily true. Now consider the proposition 'God exists'. Is this analytic? No (but see below). It is therefore not a necessary truth. From this, it follows that it is possible that God does not exist. So premise (2a) of the modal atheistic argument is true. Now consider 'God does not exist'. Is this analytic? No. So it is not a necessary truth, in which case it is possible that God does exist, and premise (2) of the modal ontological argument is true. So, if all necessary truths are analytic, then both (2) and (2a) are true. Now, if both are true, then (1) cannot be true, because (1), (2) and (2a) together imply that God both does, and does not, exist. So either we reject (1), or we reject the idea that all necessary truths are analytic.

Here is another way of reaching that conclusion. We said above that the first premise was really equivalent to the assertion that God is either necessary or impossible. Now, if necessary truth/falsehood is just analytic truth/falsehood, then 'God is either necessary or impossible' is equivalent to 'The proposition "God exists" is either analytically true or analytically false'. But 'God exists' is neither analytically true nor analytically false, so either (1) is false, or there can be necessary truths which are not analytic. Now, if there can be necessary truths which are not analytic, then we can no longer say which of (2) and (2a) is true.

But have we been too hasty here? Perhaps 'God exists' *is* analytically true (or analytically false). In fact, the ontological argument – in both the Anselmian and modal versions – would, if sound, establish that 'God exists' is analytically true. Unfortunately, the Anselmian argument fails, as we have seen, and the soundness of the modal argument is precisely what is here at issue. So the theist needs some other reason for thinking that 'God exists' is analytically true. But, if that reason is a good reason, then the ontological argument is redundant. What of the atheist's position? Some atheists do, in fact, hold that 'God exists' is analytically false. But, again, if their reasons are good ones, then the modal atheistic argument above is redundant.

In summary, then, we have the following possibilities:

1 'God exists' is analytically true, for reasons other than those provided by the modal ontological argument, so the modal ontological argument is redundant.
2 'God exists' is analytically false, so premise (2) of the modal ontological argument is false.
3 'God exists' is neither analytically true nor analytically false, and since necessary truth *is* the same as analytic truth, premise (1) is false.
4 Necessary truth is *not* the same as analytic truth, so we simply cannot say whether it is possible that God exists or that it is possible that God does not exist. In other words, we do not know if it is the modal ontological argument, or the modal atheistic argument, which is sound.

The one possibility that we can rule out is that the modal ontological argument is both sound *and* a non-redundant argument for the existence of God. Clearly, then, the theist cannot depend on it to provide a defence of his position.

## GOD AND MODAL REALISM

So far, we have explored the idea of God as a necessary being, but without settling the issue of what necessity really is. The kind of necessity at issue here is logical necessity – i.e., the strongest kind of necessity there is. Arguably, only a logically necessary being requires no explanation for its existence. Of a contingent being, we can ask why it exists when it might not have existed. Of a necessary being, we cannot ask this question, since it is not true that it might not have existed. But what is a logically necessary being? So far, we have defined necessarily true propositions as those which could not possibly be false, i.e. they are true in all possible worlds. But what is the relationship between necessarily true propositions and necessary *beings* or objects? Does the idea of a necessary being even make sense? And what, exactly, are possible worlds? We were content to use them as a device in stating arguments and articulating objections, but without making it clear what talk of possible worlds corresponds to. In this section of the chapter, we will explore these questions, and see whether one particular theory of necessity raises any interesting theological problems.

On one view, which we will call the *linguistic theory*, necessity is simply a feature of language. There are certain statements whose truth we are committed to simply because of the words we are using. Thus, for example, 'No herbivore eats meat' is necessarily true because of what 'herbivore' means. Nothing could be called a herbivore if it ate meat. Such a proposition is analytically true in both of the senses defined in Chapter 1, pages 10–11; that is, it is true in virtue of the meanings of the words, and any denial of it would involve a contradiction. Now, according to the linguistic theory, *all* necessary truths are analytic – an idea we encountered above. It is a mistake, on this view, to think of necessity as somehow characteristic of the world itself, for necessity just belongs to descriptions, not to what is described. Talk of possible worlds, in consequence, really adds nothing of any value. It explains nothing that cannot be explained in terms of the properties of language. What, then, of the characterisation of God as a necessary being? The linguistic theory, if it is to make any sense of this characterisation, must take it as equivalent to the assertion that 'The proposition "God exists" is analytically true'.

Now, as we have seen, theists have some reason to think of God as a necessary being, in that such a being seems to fill the role of providing an ultimate explanation for a merely contingent universe, one which does not immediately invite the question 'And what explains why *that* being exists rather than not?' But this does not commit the theist to the idea that 'God exists' is analytically true. Perhaps it involves no contradiction to suppose that God might not exist. Nevertheless, the theist could insist, it is still necessarily true that God exists. Such a conception is a rejection of the linguistic theory, for it admits some necessary truths which are not analytic. 'God exists' is necessarily true, we could say, but not because of the meaning of the word 'God'. It is necessarily true because it refers to a state of affairs which is necessary, one which could not have been otherwise. That is, something *in reality* confers necessity on the statement.

If we take this line, we shall have at some stage to answer the question, what in reality confers necessity on statements? It is all very well to say that a proposition is necessarily true because it refers to a state of affairs which is necessary, but this still leaves us with an unexplained notion of necessity. So let us look again at possible worlds. Are these, after all, something rather more than a useful idiom? According to *modal realism*, they are much more than a useful idiom: they are part of reality. The modal realist sees this world as just one of a number of equally real and concrete possible worlds. We cannot, however, get to these other worlds because of their complete spatial and temporal separation from us. That is, this world bears no temporal or spatial relations to any other world. No time in this world is earlier than, simultaneous with, or later than, any time in any other world. No place in this world is any distance from any place in any other world. This isolation of worlds from each other is what makes two worlds distinct. It also tells us what it is for two things to be in the same world: they stand in spatial and temporal relations to each other. Thus we belong to the same world as Napoleon and Gandhi. We do not belong to the same world as Nicholas Nickleby and the Minotaur, though they, being possible beings, are just as real as we are.

Modal realism tells us what possibilities are: they are states of affairs which obtain in other worlds. A necessary state of affairs is one which obtains in every possible world. Modal realism also makes clear what, in reality, makes propositions necessarily true or necessarily false. However, it does present some difficulties for the idea that some of the properties of objects are accidental. It is accidental that I have the property of being a writer of philosophy, in the sense that I could have been something else instead. The way we formulated this in the language of possible worlds was to say that, in some possible world, I am not a writer of philosophy. This implies that I exist in more than one world. But, if modal realism is correct, we cannot exist in more than one world, as we are bound in time and space to this one. If A is spatially and temporally unrelated to B, then they cannot be one and the same object. But if A is in one world and B is in another, then they *are* spatially and temporally unrelated to each other. Hence no-one can be in more than one world. The solution adopted by the modal realist is to say that, although I do not exist in any world but this one, I do have *counterparts* in other worlds: that is, individuals who are very like me in certain respects but different in others. Thus, I have a counterpart in some other world who is more like me than any other object in that world, but who, unlike me, is the Tsar of Russia. It is by virtue of my having in some other world a counterpart who is the

Tsar of Russia which makes it true that *I* could have been the Tsar of Russia.

Unfortunately, this raises problems for the notion of a necessary being, for a necessary being would be one which existed in all worlds. Since any being can inhabit one world at most, there is, on the modal realist picture, no such thing as a necessary being. We are assuming here, however, that everything that exists does so in time and space. Can this assumption be questioned? Perhaps a necessary being is one which does not exist in time and space. But this creates difficulties for the modal realist's notion of what it is to be in a world. If to be in a world is to be in the space and time of that world, then beings outside time and space exist in no worlds. And since the sum of all possible worlds is all there is to reality, a being which is in no world is not real. Worse, it is an *impossible* being.

What consequences does this have for God? It seems, if the modal realist picture is correct, that the theist faces a dilemma, for, either God exists in time and space, or he exists outside time and space (otherwise he does not exist at all). If he exists in time and space, then he cannot exist in more than one world. Therefore he is not a necessary being. If, however, he exists outside time and space, then he cannot exist in any world at all. Therefore he is an impossible being. Either way, it seems we cannot keep the idea of a necessary God compatibly with modal realism.

The theist may, however, defend the idea of a necessary God as follows. Although nothing can exist in more than one world, still there could in every world exist a being who is omnipotent, omniscient and perfectly good. That is, there is *a* God in every world, even though it is not the same God. Gods in other worlds are counterparts of the actual God. It is in this sense that 'God exists' is a necessary truth. This solution is certainly coherent, and it preserves something at least of the idea of a necessary God, but it is hardly a satisfactory outcome. What, for example, could be the object of worship? Either something whose existence is contingent (the God who inhabits this world), or a fragmentary being (the collection of God-counterparts in all possible worlds). Either way, it does not seem that the object of worship is a unitary, necessary object. Further, God is supposed by the theist to be the being upon which the whole of reality depends. Now the God who exists in this, the actual world, is not that being, for at most he is responsible for the existence of just this world, and there are an infinite number of other worlds which comprise reality. Similarly, no counterpart of God is a being on which the whole of reality depends. And if we point to the aggregate of God-counterparts, then again we are not identifying a single being.

Now it is not just the idea of God as a logically necessary being for which modal realism raises difficulties. Even if he is only a contingent being, we still want to talk about God in the context of non-actual but possible situations. Or we may want to say, as theists do say, that God is necessarily omnipotent, omniscient and perfectly good, that these are essential properties of God. In the idiom of possible worlds, God is omniscient, omnipotent and perfectly good in every world in which he exists. But this implies that God exists in more than one world. The modal realist's construal of this notion as God having counterparts in other worlds will not be satisfactory to the theist, for the reasons given above.

All this may not so much put pressure on the theist, as bring out difficulties in the modal realist's position. Perhaps the idea of counterparts is objectionable anyway (although I have tried to show that it is particularly objectionable to the theist). It is certainly true to say that modal realism has some unpalatable consequences, for, if every possibility is realised, albeit not in a single possible world, then we have to accept the reality, not just of an all-powerful benevolent God, but also of a series of malevolent Gods, apathetic Gods and ineffectual Gods. Modal realism supports a version of theism, but it is a theism of a particularly grotesque kind.

If modal realism is to be rejected, then we have to abandon one attempt to explain how it is that necessity can be part of the world, and not merely a feature of language. In the next chapter I shall suggest that, even if we grant the notion of a necessary being to the theist, this notion cannot play the causally explanatory role that it promises to play.

## SUMMARY

The ontological argument attempts to establish the existence of God simply by an analysis of the meaning of 'God'. Two versions of the argument were examined in this chapter. The first of these was formulated by St Anselm, and defines God as 'That than which nothing greater can be conceived'. The argument depends upon the premise that something existing in reality is greater than something which merely exists in the mind. We discovered that, once it is made clear what it is to compare something existing in reality with something existing only in the mind, the premise turns out to be false. The second argument is a modal version, making explicit use of the notion of necessity, and begins with the premise that God cannot be a merely contingent being: if it is possible for him to exist, then he necessarily exists. The difficulties with this argument are rather complex, but they revolve around the issue of whether necessary truth is the same thing as analytic truth. If it is, then this creates problems for the first premise. If it is not, then we have no way of establishing the truth of the premise that God's existence is at least possible.

In exploring the notion of necessity, the idiom of possible worlds was introduced, and, although this was a useful idiom, it was shown that a realist interpretation of it, i.e. one which posits other possible worlds as real, was in tension with traditional theism.

## FURTHER READING

A good source for Anselm's writings on the ontological argument, together with critical essays, is John Hick and A.C. McGill (eds), *The Many-faced Argument: Recent Studies on the Ontological Argument for the Existence of God*, London: Macmillan, 1968. A different version of the argument can be found in the fifth of Descartes' *Meditations*. See Donald A. Cress (ed.), *René Descartes, Discourse on Method and Meditations on First Philosophy*, 3rd Edition, Indianapolis: Hackett Publishing Company, 1993.

For an introductory discussion of Anselm's argument, see William L. Rowe, *Philosophy of Religion: An Introduction*, Belmont: Wadsworth Publishing Company, 1978, Chapter 3. An extended treatment is provided by Jonathan Barnes, *The Ontological Argument*, London: Macmillan, 1972.

A modal version of the argument, which is somewhat more complex than the one examined in this chapter, though the underlying moves are essentially the same, is presented and defended by Alvin Plantinga, in *The Nature of Necessity*, Oxford: Clarendon Press, 1974, Chapter 10. Plantinga also discusses Anselm's argument, and casts it in the idiom of possible worlds. Both arguments are criticised in detail by John Mackie, in Chapter 3 of *The Miracle of Theism*, Oxford: Oxford University Press, 1982.

An accessible summary of various approaches to modal discourse is provided by Stephen Read's *Thinking About Logic*, Oxford: Oxford University Press, 1994, Chapter 4. David Lewis is the acknowledged originator of realism about possible worlds, and he provides a detailed and sophisticated defence of modal realism in *On the Plurality of Worlds*, Oxford: Blackwell, 1986. Physical arguments in favour of the 'many universes' theory – the physicist's counterpart of modal realism – are briefly reviewed in P.C.W. Davies, *The Accidental Universe*, Cambridge: Cambridge University Press, 1982.

# 3 Could the universe have an explanation?

> ... we believe that no fact can be real or existing and no statement true or false
> unless it has a sufficient reason why it should be thus and not otherwise. Most
> frequently, however, these reasons cannot be known by us.
>
> Gottfried Wilhelm von Leibniz, *Monadology*

## A TRIVIAL EXPLANATION

We began the first chapter with the observation that theism appears to
explain why the universe exists, and that there appears, moreover, to be
no rival explanation. The implicit assumption is that the existence of the
universe is something to be explained. But is it to be explained? Is theism,
rather, making a mistake in attempting an explanation? In this chapter
we shall discuss two arguments: one that the existence of the universe can
be explained in quite trivial terms, which make no reference to God; and
the other that there cannot be a causal explanation, or anything even
analogous to a causal explanation, of the existence of the universe.

First, the trivial explanation. By this point we have become quite
familiar with talk of possible worlds. I now want to show that such talk
allows us to construct a very simple, indeed disappointingly simple,
answer to our fundamental question, 'Why does the universe exist?'
However, to see how the explanation works, we have to rephrase our
question as follows: 'Why is the actual world one which contains a
universe?' The 'explanation' now goes as follows. The set of all possible
worlds represents the full range of logical possibility. Anything that is
logically possible will be true in some possible world or worlds. The
existence of a universe is clearly possible, since it is actual. Consequently,
some possible worlds contain a universe, even though many do not.
Whenever the phrase 'The actual world' is used by us, it denotes the
world we happen to be in, just as whenever we use the word 'here' it
denotes the place we happen to be in. So the question 'Why is this world

one which contains a universe?' just means 'Why is the world in which I am located one which contains a universe?', and that question hardly seems to deserve an answer. For, of course, the world in which I am located is bound to be a world which contains a universe. The very posing of the question presupposes the answer.

A simple analogy may help to make this argument intelligible. Imagine that you are sitting in one of a hundred rooms in some office building. Some of these rooms are occupied, some not. Reflecting on this, you ask yourself, 'Why is *this* room an occupied room?' The answer is not hard to find. Consider the meaning of 'this room'. Which room is referred to by 'this room' obviously depends on the location of the speaker. As we might put it, 'this room' just means 'The room where I am located'. So the question 'Why is this room occupied?' just means 'Why is the room in which I am located an occupied room?' and the absurdity of the question is at once apparent. Any room in which I am located is *ipso facto* an occupied room, so in that sense the fact that this room is occupied needs no explanation beyond a brief summary of what is meant by the phrase 'this room'. Similarly, the fact that the actual world contains a universe is answered quite trivially, by a summary of what is meant by 'the actual world'.

If this is the correct explanation, then any further explanation is redundant. Theism, as far as the mystery of existence is concerned, is simply *de trop*. But the 'explanation', of course, is too good to be true. What is wrong with it? We might note that the explanation in terms of the meaning of 'this room' does not rule out an informative explanation of why this room is an occupied one. I can explain why this room is occupied by pointing to the fact that I have just walked into it, having been asked by someone to find a file. But what is particularly suspicious about the trivial explanation is the analogy between the office building and the totality of possible worlds. There is nothing, apart from their contents, to distinguish one room from any other of the ninety-nine rooms in the block. By this I do not mean that they are all of the same dimensions, or similarly furnished, but that each is as *real* as the other. 'This room' is just the room I happen to be in. But *this world* is, surely, very different from all the other possible worlds. This world, the actual world, is *the real* world; all others are just fantasies, mere abstract possibilities. We can agree that 'this room' and 'here' make implicit reference to the speaker, but 'the actual world' surely makes no such reference. So the question 'Why does the actual world contain a universe?' is not the dubious question 'Why does the world in which I am located contain a universe?', but 'Why does the one world which is real contain a universe?', a question which has nothing to do with the individual posing the question. To answer *this* question surely requires a substantive explanation.

There is, however, a theory on which the analogy between worlds and the office building is an appropriate one, and that is the modal realist theory discussed in Chapter 2, pages 29–31. On that view, all worlds are equally real, and the actual world is merely the one we happen to be located in. So, if modal realism is correct, then there really is no mystery about the existence of the universe. Here is one of many instances where modal realism creates difficulties for theism. But the price to pay for the solution to the mystery is a very high one: a controversial and counter-intuitive conception of reality. If we keep to our intuitive conception of possibility, then the mystery cannot be got rid of so easily. The point is, then, that it is not just the useful idiom of possible worlds that defuses the fundamental questions of existence, but a controversial interpretation of that idiom. However, there is another argument, to the effect that the existence of the universe has no substantial explanation, and to this argument we now turn.

## CAUSES AND CAUSAL EXPLANATIONS

Our discussion of the cosmological argument showed us that the notion of an uncaused *cause* of the universe is a dubious one. But the theist can still exploit our puzzlement over the idea of something's coming into being from nothing. The universe still needs an explanation. And, even though a 'cause' of the universe would necessarily be very different from ordinary causes, it nevertheless offers something at least analogous to a causal explanation of the universe. In so far as we think the universe needs an explanation, then, we will be tempted by theism. What I want to suggest now, however, is that, although theism can point to a cause of the universe, in an extended sense of 'cause', it cannot provide anything like a causal *explanation* of the universe. This might seem a curious assertion. After all, what is there to causal explanation other than simply pointing to a cause? A simple example will illustrate the difference.

Suppose you observe smoke emerging from your neighbour's house and you enquire of someone in the large crowd of people gathered outside what the explanation is. If you were told that smoke was emerging from your neighbour's house because some smoke-producing event had occurred inside, then you would certainly have been told a truth, though a rather uninformative one. But if the observer had said, in place of 'smoke-producing event', 'burning of furniture', then the explanation would have been a useful, informative one: it would have told you something you could not have known simply by looking at the smoke. So we can define one feature that a good causal explanation should have: it should be genuinely informative, in the sense that it contains information not provided by the description of the effect.

Is informativeness enough? Suppose that, instead of saying either that some smoke-producing event had occurred or that there had been a burning of furniture, the observer had said that there had been a visit by relatives. This would certainly have told you something you could not have known simply by looking at the smoke, but you would have been somewhat bemused by it if you had not known that the relatives in question had in fact been disinherited and the burning of the furniture was an act of defiance on their part. There is in the world at large no general connection between visits by relatives and the production of smoke (other than tobacco smoke, that is). So the observer's reference to such a visit would not necessarily have made intelligible the appearance of smoke. Whether it would have done so would have depended on the background information of the audience. A second aspect of good causal explanation, then, is its connection with generalisations. To take another example, if we think that the fact that a flask containing a mixture of chlorine and hydrogen was exposed to sunlight explains the explosion in the laboratory, that is because we think that there is a general connection between mixtures of chlorine and hydrogen being exposed to sunlight and explosions. At its most basic, the explanation is of this kind: A explains B because A-type events are nearly always accompanied by B-type events. More complex explanations rely on a greater number of generalisations: A explains B because A-type events are generally accompanied by C-type events which in turn are generally accompanied by B-type events. For example, the exposure of the mixture to sunlight (A) explains the explosion (B) because, in the presence of sunlight, chlorine and hydrogen interact to form hydrogen chloride (C-type event), and the bonding of chlorine and hydrogen atoms releases a large amount of energy.

The point of causal explanations is to make intelligible the phenomenon in question: to make it less surprising or mysterious. When we have an explanation, we know (or at least are in a better position to know) what to expect next. But it is not enough to point to some state of affairs as the cause of some other state. The way in which the cause is described determines whether the explanation is a good one or not. Under some descriptions, the cause and effect will exemplify a general connection between events of a certain kind and events of another kind. Under other descriptions, the cause and effect will not exemplify a general connection (as it would not if, for example, we had described the cause above as 'sunlight falling on a yellow-coloured gas'). So we can define another feature of good causal explanation as follows: we should describe the causes in a way that brings out a general connection between causes of that type and events of the type exemplified by the effect. Admittedly, some causal explanations will be so complex that they cannot be generalised. But, in these cases, the explanations will depend on component explanations which do involve general connections.

Now let us look at the idea that the universe is caused by some 'first cause'. This may be perfectly correct, but as an *explanation* it is a dead loss: it tells nothing about the first cause other than that it is a cause. It is on the same level as 'smoke is coming from that house because some smoke-producing event is going on inside'. Pointing to a cause of the universe only becomes an explanation once one adds extra information about the cause, thus making the universe – and perhaps also particular features of it – intelligible. So the mere postulation of a first cause fails to meet our first requirement of a good causal explanation.

Suppose, then, that we say rather more about the first cause: we specify certain of its properties. Can we still hope to produce something like a good causal explanation of the universe? Consider our second requirement of causal explanation, that good causal explanations generate true generalisations. A world in which there can be causal explanation is not a chaotic world; it is a world tightly constrained by the laws of nature. Causal generalisations are simply reflections of these laws: that is, they are true because of the existence of fundamental laws. Causal explanation, then, takes place against a background of laws. But when we come to the explanation of the universe as a whole, part of what we are required to explain is the existence of the laws themselves. We cannot therefore help ourselves to any laws in order to explain the existence of the universe. Consequently, the explanation of the universe cannot take place against a background of laws. But, since causal explanation requires such a background, there can be no causal explanation of the universe.

Many philosophers insist on a connection between laws and causation itself. That is, quite independently of any considerations about explanation, two things cannot be related as cause and effect unless there are laws connecting one type of event with the other. This might seem to imply, for reasons similar to those discussed in the previous paragraph, that there could not be a *cause* of the universe, never mind a causal explanation. For, it might seem, if causation requires laws, and whatever is responsible for the universe is responsible for the laws themselves, then that thing cannot be a cause in the ordinary sense. But, to get around this difficulty, the theist can distinguish between natural and non-natural laws. The natural laws are those which govern causation within the universe, and whose existence requires explanation. The non-natural laws are those which connect God's activity with the existence of the universe. Admittedly, we cannot have an access to the non-natural laws, but that in itself does not prevent us from talking of a cause of the universe's existence. It does, however, prevent us from talking of a causal *explanation* of the universe's existence, since we can only make things intelligible by appealing to things of which we know. Causal explanation is thus tied to the natural laws.

The possibility remains, however, of a different kind of explanation of the universe, one which does not depend on natural laws. This suggestion has been made by Richard Swinburne, who argues that there is a kind of explanation which is very familiar to us, which is independent of scientific explanation in terms of natural laws, and to which the theist can appeal in explaining both the existence and characteristics of the universe. He calls it *personal explanation*.

## PERSONAL EXPLANATION

In *The Existence of God*, Swinburne defines personal explanation as explanation in terms of an agent and that agent's intentions. For example, I explain the presence of the lawnmower in the kitchen by saying that I put it there the previous evening with the intention that it should remind me, when I came down to breakfast, to take it to be mended. Nothing could be more familiar than this kind of explanation. It belongs to the category of *teleological* explanation – explanation in terms of purpose – rather than that of causal explanation. In causal explanation, we point to the antecedents of something. A causal explanation of the presence of the lawnmower may involve a simple description of my actions the evening before: I took it out of the garden shed, I opened the kitchen door... etc. A more detailed causal explanation might include a description of my individual body movements, and the brain processes which gave rise to those movements. In teleological explanation, in contrast, we point, not solely to the antecedents of something, but to its goal, the end to which it is tending. The teleological explanation of the lawnmower's being in the kitchen, in terms of what I wanted to achieve, is intelligible quite independently of any detailed causal explanation. Moreover, the teleological explanation does something the causal explanation does not: it rationalises my action of bringing the lawnmower into the kitchen. As we shall see in Chapter 5, however, not all teleological explanation must involve conscious agents, so not all teleological explanation is personal.

Theism, and only theism, offers a personal explanation of the universe. The theist can say why the universe exists by saying that it was brought about by God, who intended that there should be a universe. Or perhaps the main intention was to realise some state of affairs for which the existence of a universe was a necessary condition. Surely this meets the requirements of good explanation? It is informative, and it rests on general principles concerning how rational agents behave. The question is whether we can legitimately extend this familiar form of explanation to the case of the universe.

The crucial notion in personal explanation is that of *intention*. Now, as we ordinarily encounter them, intentions are the causes of actions. This is not to say that explanation in terms of intentions is just causal explanation. As we noted above, they are different in form and play different roles in our understanding. Still, intentions are *causes*: they are had by the agent at certain times and not others, and they bring about the effect in question in conjunction with other conditions. Swinburne objects to this on the grounds that intentions are not, or at least not always, 'occurrent' mental events: they are not happenings which take place at particular times and of which we are fully conscious, like a sudden surge of pain. But we do not have to think of intentions as occurrent events in order to see them as causes. We could think of them as dispositions to behave in certain ways. My intention to be nice to people may not be at the forefront of my mind, it may not be something I consciously decided to adopt one day. It is simply something about me which is manifested in my behaviour towards people. It is still a cause (though not the only cause) of my behaviour: it is a condition which has not always obtained, but which does obtain antecedently to the behaviour in question.

If intentions are causes in the ordinary sense of the term, then the suggestion that a creator's intentions could explain the existence of the universe implies that the universe had a cause. In Chapter 1 we argued that, when we consider the causes of the existence of things, it is an essential part of our notion of those causes that they bear a temporal relationship to the things they cause. They occur, or obtain, immediately before the thing in question comes into existence. Now, if the universe had no beginning, and so there was no time before it existed, then it cannot have had a cause. Equally, if it had a beginning, but this coincided with the beginning of time, then there still would have been no time before the universe began to exist, so it cannot have had a cause. In these cases, then, we cannot appeal to an antecedent intention to explain why the universe came into existence, if intentions are causes. We left the door open at the end of Chapter 1 for an extended, non-standard, use of the term 'cause', but it is far from clear that we can conceive of an intention which is a cause only in some non-standard sense.

If the universe had a beginning, but time did not, then we could allow that the universe had a cause. So, in such a case, personal explanation would be applicable, it seems. There is, however, another problem, to which I shall now turn.

## A NECESSARY CAUSE?

The first premise of the modal cosmological argument is that everything whose existence is contingent has a cause. This suggests that, if there were a first cause, it would be necessarily existent. Now we can state this in terms of explanation as follows. Every contingent fact, e.g. the fact that the universe exists, calls for causal explanation. If there is an ultimate explanation, a fact which calls for no further explanation, then it must be a necessary fact, one which obtains in all worlds. The fact in question may be that God exists, or that he has certain properties. Let us suppose, then, that the fact which causally explains the universe is a necessary one. But this will not do. Since the very problem was to explain why the *actual* world, but not all worlds, contained a universe, i.e. what it was about this particular world that made the crucial difference, appeal to a feature which all worlds share will not advance our understanding any further at all. Even if a necessary fact is an important part of the explanation, it cannot be the whole of it.

Necessary facts, then, cannot explain contingent ones, and causal explanation, of any phenomenon, must link contingent facts. That is, both cause and effect must be contingent. Why is this? Because causes make a difference to their environment: they result in something that would not have happened if the cause had not been present. To say, for example, that the presence of a catalyst in a certain set of circumstances speeded up a reaction is to say that, had the catalyst not been present in those circumstances, the reaction would have proceeded at a slower rate. In general, if A caused B, then, if A had not occurred in the circumstances, B would not have occurred either. (A variant of this principle is that, if A caused B, then if A had not occurred in the circumstances, the probability of B's occurrence would have been appreciably less than it was. It does not matter for our argument whether we accept the original principle or this variant.) To make sense of this statement, 'If A had not occurred in the circumstances, B would not have occurred', we have to countenance the possibility of A's not occurring and the possibility of B's not occurring. If these are genuine possibilities, then both A and B are contingent. So one of the reasons why necessary facts cannot causally explain anything is that we cannot make sense of their not being the case, whereas causal explanation requires us to make sense of causally explanatory facts not being the case. Causal explanation involves the explanation of one contingent fact by appeal to another contingent fact.

This means that we cannot solve our problem by giving up the contingency of the universe. That is, we cannot say that, since no contingent fact could explain the universe, and since no necessary fact explains a contingent one, the existence of the universe is both itself a necessary fact and explained by a necessary fact. If the existence of the universe is necessary, not contingent, then it seems it does not call for explanation. Or rather, it cannot have a *causal* explanation, for the reasons just given.

These considerations also affect any attempted personal explanation of the universe, for, as we argued in the previous section, intentions are causes – and, since causes are contingent, so are intentions. Therefore, any personal explanation of the universe in terms of the intentions of a creator must also be contingently true. So, if the contingency of the universe is what makes us seek an explanation for it, the contingency of personal explanation will also invite the request for further explanation. *Why* did the creator have such intentions? If the theist insists that this is one contingent fact that we cannot explain further, then the original motivation for explaining the existence of the universe is undermined, for the atheist can insist that the existence of the universe is a contingent fact that we cannot explain further.

If something is forcing us to seek an explanation for the existence or nature of the universe, it must be something stronger than the mere fact that things could have been otherwise, for any explanation will only invoke things that could have been otherwise. However, there is another reason to seek an explanation of the universe, and that is to do with the notion of *probability*. This aspect of the mysteries of existence is one of the concerns of the next chapter.

## SUMMARY

The argument of this chapter has been that, once it is made clear what counts as a satisfactory causal explanation of anything, it becomes apparent that there can be no causal explanation, worthy of the name 'explanation', of why the universe exists.

We began by looking at the suggestion that the explanation of the universe's existence is a trivial one, and therefore any causal explanation would simply be redundant. The argument went as follows: the question

'Why is the actual world one which contains a universe?' is just equivalent to 'Why is the world in which *I* am located one which contains a universe?', a question which invites the obvious answer that any world which contains me must also contain a universe. We saw, however, that this argument rested on the very controversial step of treating other possible worlds as being as real as the actual world.

We then turned to the question of whether there could be a causal explanation, or something at least analogous to a causal explanation, of the universe, and distinguished between simply pointing to a cause and providing a genuine explanation. Three features of causal explanation were identified:

1  Good causal explanations are informative.
2  Good causal explanations exploit generalisations of the following form: A-type events tend to cause, in certain situations, B-type events. Under some descriptions, but not others, a cause and effect will fall under this kind of generalisation.
3  If some state of affairs, B, has a cause, then both B and its cause are contingent: if it is true that A caused B, then if in the circumstances A had not occurred, B would not have occurred.

The first of these entails that merely positing a first cause of the universe is not explanatory; the third entails that no necessary fact could provide a causal explanation of the universe; and the second generates the following argument: causal explanations require a background of laws, but an explanation of the existence of the universe cannot presuppose such a background since the existence of laws is part of what it is required to explain, hence there can be nothing even approaching a causal explanation of the existence of the universe.

A different possibility was explored: that the universe could be given a personal explanation in terms of the intentions of a creator. This is a different kind of explanation from causal explanation, and so does not face all the difficulties of the latter. Nevertheless, if intentions are causes, then personal explanation implies that there was a cause of the universe, and this faces the difficulties raised in Chapter 1. Further, personal explanation is contingent, and so, if it is the contingency of the universe which obliges us to seek an explanation for it, personal explanation simply invites a regress of explanation.

## FURTHER READING

The modal realist solution to the fundamental questions of existence is made explicit in David Lewis's *On the Plurality of Worlds*, Oxford:

Blackwell, 1986, pp. 128–33. See also George Schlesinger, 'Possible Worlds and the Mystery of Existence', *Ratio*, vol. 26 (1984), pp. 1–17.

Theories of causation, and the connection between causation and laws, are discussed in detail in John Mackie, *The Cement of the Universe*, Oxford: Clarendon Press, 1974.

The notion of personal explanation is articulated and put to use in a defence of theism in Richard Swinburne's *The Existence of God*, Oxford: Clarendon Press, 1979.

For a detailed characterisation of explanation in its various guises see David-Hillel Ruben, *Explaining Explanation*, London: Routledge, 1990.

# 4 Are we the outcome of chance or design?

To understand God's thoughts we must study statistics, for these are the measure of his purpose.

Attributed to Florence Nightingale

## ANALOGY AND THE TELEOLOGICAL ARGUMENT

Whereas the various versions of the cosmological argument start from relatively general observations about the universe, teleological arguments for God's existence start with more specific observations: for example, that the universe is highly ordered, or that living things are well adapted to their environments. Another difference between the two kinds of arguments is that, whereas for the cosmological argument the crucial notion is that of causality, for the teleological argument the crucial notion is that of *purpose*. We can make the existence of something intelligible by pointing to its antecedent cause, or we can make intelligible its existence by pointing to the purpose for which it was made, provided of course that we are talking of artefacts, i.e. things which are constructed by a conscious agent. The teleological argument for God is that naturally occurring features of the universe were constructed by a conscious agent with a certain end in mind. It is this aspect that gives the argument its name, for the Greek word *telos* means 'end' or 'goal'.

The period in which the teleological argument, in its original form, was most influential was undoubtedly the eighteenth century. The developing sciences of astronomy, chemistry and biology – particularly the last of these – provided a wealth of examples of highly ordered systems whose complexity made it almost inconceivable that they could have been the outcome of chance. This gave rise to a new justification of theism, based on the idea that the path to belief was not through revelation, but rather through the contemplation of the wonders of the natural world. The teleological argument was presented in terms of an analogy between various naturally occurring things – in particular, parts of living things – and human artefacts. Perhaps the most famous example of the analogy was the one articulated by William Paley: just as a watch is a complex mechanism, having parts which cooperate so as to achieve a certain end, namely the measurement of time, so, for example, the eye is a (highly) complex system, having parts which cooperate so as to achieve a series of ends, such as providing information about its environment to the organism. The watch bears *marks of design*: the fact that it can be used for the purpose of measuring time suggests that it was devised by an intelligence with that purpose in mind. Similarly, the eye bears (what can be interpreted to be) marks of design: the fact that it can be used for seeing suggests that it was devised by an intelligence with that purpose in mind. That living things are as they are is testimony to the existence of a creator.

That, in a nutshell, is the traditional teleological argument. Since the universe is full of apparent 'marks of design', the argument may take as its first premise any of a number of observations about the universe, each supposedly requiring a creator to explain it. Some teleological arguments, for example, started from observations about the solar system. One version drew an analogy between the entire universe and a machine. Here is how the analogy is presented by Cleanthes, one of the fictional participants in Hume's *Dialogues Concerning Natural Religion*:

> Look round the world, contemplate the whole and every part of it: you will find it to be nothing but one great machine, subdivided into an infinite number of lesser machines, which again admit of subdivisions to a degree beyond what human senses and faculties can trace and explain. All these machines, and even their most minute parts, are adjusted to each other with an accuracy which ravishes into admiration all men who have ever contemplated them. The curious adapting of means to ends, throughout all nature, resembles exactly, though it much exceeds, the productions of human contrivance...
>
> (Hume 1779, Part II)

The notion of purpose was, however, more obviously applied to the parts of living things. The parts of the body clearly do have a function: the legs, or wings, for locomotion, the stomach for digestion, the circulatory system for the transport of gases and dissolved nutrients, etc. Does the fitness of the parts to their ends, and more generally the adaptation of living things to their environment, not indicate the existence of a creator who so constructed them? This rhetorical question, however, highlights the fact that the traditional teleological argument has not survived the advance of science. We now know, or think we know, why life is adapted to its environment: by the production of thousands of variations, some of which will better adapt the organism which has them to its environment and which will therefore provide it with a better chance of survival. Evolution through natural selection is the non-theological account of what, prior to Darwin, seemed an extraordinary fact requiring the hypothesis of a benevolent creator to explain it. The appearance of design, then, may simply be specious. Although we can, at one level, talk of the purpose of the eye – to provide information about the immediate environment – the facts underlying this talk are not themselves purposive. It is not that the eye developed in order that organisms would be all the better at adapting themselves to their environment, but rather that the adaptive consequences of having eyes ensured that the organisms possessing them would be more likely to reproduce. (This 'reductionist' account will be looked at more closely in the next chapter.)

The analogy between artefacts and sense organs is a weak one, therefore. Although there are no laws which would explain the natural (i.e. non-artificial) production of accurate mechanical time pieces, there are laws which explain the natural development of sense organs.

## PROBABILITY AND THE TELEOLOGICAL ARGUMENT

However, this is not the demise of the teleological argument, for, instead of focusing on the results of the laws of nature, we can focus on the laws themselves and ask why these laws, ones which permitted the evolution of life in the universe, should have been the ones to dictate what happened. The occurrence of life on earth seems to have depended upon some remarkably improbable features of the physical universe. For example, life as we know it is carbon-based: most of the important chemicals constituting the bodies of organisms are complex molecules in which carbon atoms join to form long chains. Where did this carbon come from? The currently favoured answer is that it is synthesised in large quantities in stars, and it was from the explosion of a star that the present universe was formed. But the fact that carbon is synthesised in significant quantities in stars depends upon two apparent coincidences. One concerns the relationship between the thermal energy of the nuclear constituents of stars and a property of the carbon nucleus; the other concerns the relationship between this same thermal energy and a property of the oxygen nucleus. Without the first relationship, little carbon would have been formed in stars in the first place, since not enough energy would have been available to form it. Without the second relationship, what carbon was formed would have been converted, through bombardment by helium, into oxygen, because too much energy would have been produced. Either way, carbon-based life would not have developed. If this is to be regarded as a coincidence, it is, it seems, a remarkably improbable one. How much more probable, says the contemporary teleologist, that the initial conditions of the universe were so arranged that the development of life as we know it was possible.

What we have here is a modern teleological argument, differing from the original form in two respects. First, the marks of design are to be looked for not in living things but in the fundamental constants: i.e. in basic physical values, such as the atomic mass of oxygen, which remain the same in all places and at all times; second, the reasoning is probabilistic rather than analogical: instead of drawing comparisons between artefacts and creation, the argument stresses the improbability of the coincidences to which atheism commits us. The analogy between the created order and human artefacts remains, but it is no longer required to bear the weight of the argument. The modern teleological argument is not an argument *from* analogy, but rather *to* analogy: it is because we are justified in positing a creator that we are justified in drawing an analogy between certain aspects of the universe and human artefacts.

Let us now spell out the probabilistic reasoning more explicitly. The argument appeals to the following principle: we have good reason to believe that some hypothesis is a true explanation of some phenomenon if (i) the probability of the phenomenon's occurring given that the hypothesis is true is much greater than the probability of its occurring given that the hypothesis is false, *and* (ii) if the hypothesis is true, then the probability of the phenomenon's occurring is much greater than the probability of its not occurring. This seems sensible enough, indeed it could be a rule for the rational scientist. How does it favour theism? The fact that, given theism, it was much more probable that the initial conditions would favour the development of life than that they would not, and the fact that the hypothesis of theism makes the life-favouring initial conditions of the universe vastly more probable than they would have been had theism been false, provide us with powerful arguments in favour of theism. (I am calling these 'facts', but whether they really are so is something we shall need to examine.) We can now set out the modern, probabilistic teleological argument in full as follows:

*The probabilistic teleological argument*

1  The laws of the universe are such as to permit the development of life.

2  The probability of (1)'s being true on the hypothesis that there is a God who desires the development of life is much greater than

the probability of (1)'s being true on the hypothesis that there is no such God.

3  If there does exist a God who desires the development of life, then the probability of (1)'s being true is much greater than the probability of its being false.

4  We have good reason to believe that some hypothesis is a true explanation of some phenomenon if (i) the probability of the phenomenon's occurring given that the hypothesis is true is much greater than the probability of its occurring given that the hypothesis is false, *and* (ii) if the hypothesis is true, then the probability of the phenomenon's occurring is much greater than the probability of its not occurring.

*Therefore:* We have good reason to believe that there is a God who desires the development of life.

If we are looking for an argument for a God who is recognisably the God of traditional theism, then the teleological argument takes us much further along the road than does the cosmological argument, because, whereas the latter only posits a cause for the universe without providing us with a reason for thinking of it as an *intelligent* cause, the former points to something which has intentions, for example the intention to bring about the evolution of life in the universe.

The teleological argument fills another gap in the case for theism. As we remarked at the end of the previous chapter, if it is only the *contingency* of the universe, or its features, which leads us to seek further explanation, then our search will be endless, for each contingent explanation will require further explanation. But the probabilistic argument suggests that it is the apparent *improbability* of the universe's being as it is which should incline us to look for an explanation, an explanation which would make it less improbable.

We might pause for a moment, before going on to assess the argument, to note that the conclusion of the teleological argument, as we have set it out, is quite different in form from that of the cosmological and ontological arguments. Those arguments have as their conclusion the proposition that God exists, whereas the probabilistic teleological argument has as its conclusion the weaker proposition that *we have good reason to believe* that God exists. If we are trying to construct a valid argument from probabilistic considerations, this is inevitable. There will always be a gap between what it is reasonable to believe and what is true. We may be perfectly justified in adopting a hypothesis, having correctly applied reliable principles of probabilistic reasoning, and yet that hypothesis turn out to be false. But the conclusion of the argument is still highly significant, and, if the argument is a good one, then we have what all but the most sceptical would count as an adequate defence of theism.

## THE CONCEPT OF CHANCE

The probabilistic argument is valid. But are its premises true? Let us look first at the principle set out in premise (4):

4 We have good reason to believe that some hypothesis is a true explanation of some phenomenon if (i) the probability of the phenomenon's occurring given that the hypothesis is true is much greater than the probability of its occurring given that the hypothesis is false, *and* (ii) if the hypothesis is true, then the probability of the phenomenon's occurring is much greater than the probability of its not occurring.

Both conditions seem plausible because they describe our reasoning about everyday situations. If a lamp does not come on when the switch is operated, but all the other lights in the house are working, we will naturally assume that the bulb has blown. This is a familiar context to which the rule above obviously applies, if it applies anywhere. But the teleological argument was not concerned with a familiar context such as lights failing to come on, but rather with the context of the laws and fundamental constants of nature. Do the rules of probability still apply in this less familiar context?

When we are considering the probability of a phenomenon such as a lamp's failing to come on, we do so against a background of information. The lamp is plugged in, and switched on at the mains, a bulb is fitted, the other lights are on. We also include, in this background information, some laws of physics – for example the fact that, when electricity flows through a narrow tungsten wire in a rarefied atmosphere containing no oxygen but some argon, the wire tends to glow. (We can, if we know enough, derive this from more fundamental laws.) Given all this information, we will assume that the lamp is more likely to come on than not. However, if we add the information that there has been a power failure, then we will assume that the lamp is more likely not to come on. What determines the probability of the lamp's coming on is a conjunction of the various states of affairs obtaining and the laws of physics. Altering any of these will alter the probability. But if the probability of events is determined in part by the laws of physics, what can it mean to talk of the probability of the laws of physics themselves? If we judge that it was *extremely improbable* that the charge on the proton should have been $1 \cdot 602 \times 10^{-19}$ coulomb, against what background are we making our judgement? What do we suppose is determining the probability of this value? Not, surely, the other laws of physics, for any given law will either have nothing whatsoever to do with the charge on the proton, or otherwise will actually entail that it has the value that it has.

The difficulty here is precisely analogous to the difficulty encountered in Chapter 3, pages 37–8. There we pointed out that causal explanation takes place against a background of laws, so it is inappropriate to talk of a causal explanation of the laws themselves. Similarly, since statements of probability take place against a background of laws, it is inappropriate to talk of the probability of the laws themselves.

The defender of the teleological argument has a reply to this objection, which goes as follows. Admittedly, when we are dealing with ordinary situations, the probability of an event, such as a fire, depends upon a whole series of background conditions. Working out the probability in any detail will, in fact, be a complex process. But when we talk of the improbability of the universe's favouring life we mean something much simpler. We imagine a series of possible universes, some of which have laws which favour the development of life as we know it, but the vast majority of which will not favour life as we know it. Given that only one imaginary universe will correspond to the way things really are, it is much more probable that the one which does will be in the majority group (i.e. the life-hostile universes) than in the minority group (i.e. the life-favouring universes). However, if we hypothesise that which imaginary universe corresponds to the way things are is actually determined by a being who desires the evolution of life, then the tables are turned, and it becomes vastly more likely that the laws of the universe will be life-favouring ones. Since we know that the laws of the universe are life-favouring ones, we have a reason to suppose that there is such a being who made things turn out this way.

The concept of probability that is in play here is sometimes called *statistical probability* or *chance*. It is not the only kind of probability that there is, but it is the one most clearly relevant to this argument, and we should pause to examine it more carefully. We can illustrate statistical probability with the very familiar case of tossing a coin. Suppose we toss a coin 1,000 times and note the number of times the coin lands heads and the number of times it lands tails. Assuming that the coin is not 'loaded' in any way, and that the tosses are fair, we would expect a roughly even distribution of outcomes, i.e. 500 times heads and 500 times tails, or some approximation to this, such as 455 heads and 545 tails. The greater the number of tosses, the greater would be the approximation to 50 per cent heads and 50 per cent tails. So we say that the statistical probability (hereafter 'chance') of the coin's landing tails is 0.5.

This only tells us how chance is measured, however. It does not tell us what chance is, in the sense of providing a metaphysical account. And a metaphysical account of chance is what we need if we are to determine the legitimacy of using the concept in the context of the teleological argument. One, very influential, account is the *frequency theory*. According to the frequency theory, the chance of a given outcome is just the frequency of that outcome in a large enough sample. So, when we describe the chance of a coin's landing tails as 0.5, this is just equivalent to the assertion that in a large enough sample of tosses, 50 per cent of the tosses result in tails. Strictly, then, the frequency theorist would not allow that chance is *measured by* frequency: chance just *is* frequency. What the simple example of a coin obscures, however, is that frequency will be relative to a population. Thus the frequency of people dying within twenty years of a certain date in, for example, a population of people who were non-smoking, healthy teenagers at that date will be quite different from the frequency in a population of people who were heavy smokers, had parents who died of heart disease and were over 80 at that date. This, for the frequency theorist, is what it means to say that the chances of your having a life expectancy of twenty years will vary according to your age, medical history, life-style, etc.

However, if this is the correct account of chance, the use of it by the teleological argument is quite illegitimate. The chance, it is said, of the universe turning out to be life-supporting is vanishingly small on the atheist hypothesis. That must mean, if the frequency theory is correct, that the frequency of universes capable of sustaining life is very small in the total population of universes. But the total population of universes contains exactly one member, namely the actual universe. It would seem to follow that the chance of there being a universe capable of sustaining life is actually very high; indeed, it is 1! This cannot be right. For chance to make sense on the frequency theory, the relevant population must contain more than one member. Perhaps, then, the relevant population is the population of *possible* universes, and this is the way in which we presented the argument when we talked earlier of 'imaginary universes'. But this cannot be right either, precisely because these other universes are not real: they are not there to be counted. Of course, if modal realism is correct, then they *are* real, but the defender of the teleological argument would be ill-advised to appeal to modal realism because, as we saw in Chapter 3, pages 33–5, modal realism undercuts any substantive explanation for the existence of a life-sustaining universe.

The frequency theory suffers from two rather serious limitations, however. The first is that we do, intuitively, want a distinction between the measure of chance and chance itself. Frequency is, surely, only an indication of real chance. The second is that we want to be able to talk of chance in a single case. It is because we want to talk of chance in the single case, in fact, that we want the distinction between frequency and what it measures. Take this particular coin. It has never been tossed before and I intend to toss it just once. Do we not want to be able to say that there is a certain chance of its landing tails on that one toss? If we do say this, we do not mean, surely, just that if it were tossed enough times, the frequency of tails would be 50 per cent. Chance is, arguably, a property of the single case. It does not depend on whether the experiment is, or even could be, repeated. This is exactly what will be insisted on by the proponent of the teleological argument: although only one universe is realised, the fact that the one which is realised is capable of sustaining life has a certain chance.

So, in place of frequency theory, we may prefer *propensity theory*. Just as solubility is a disposition of a lump of sugar – the disposition to dissolve when placed in water – so, according to propensity theory, the chance of landing tails is a disposition of a coin. Some coins are fair, some are biased. The chances of their landing tails will therefore differ, and this is because of a real property of the coins themselves. This property we will call a *propensity*: a disposition which is, or determines, the chance of a certain outcome. Propensities are measurable, and frequency is what measures them. But the propensity does not depend on the actual frequency of an outcome in any population any more than solubility depends on being actually immersed in water.

It is widely thought that chance merely reflects our ignorance, and that, if we knew precisely the conditions of a given throw (the shape of the coin, the number of spins, the angle at which it hits the table, etc.), we would be able to work out whether it would land heads or tails. Or, even if we could never work it out, the initial conditions nevertheless determine the outcome, so that the *real* probability of landing tails on a given throw will in fact be either 1 or 0: i.e. it will either be necessary that it lands tails, or impossible. If everything in the world is determined in this way, it is argued, then there are in reality no probabilities between 1 and 0. The reason the frequency of tails is, in a large number of throws, 50 per cent, is simply that the conditions of each throw differ slightly from those of the other throws. If the conditions were repeated exactly in each case, then the frequency of tails would be either 1 or 0. We should therefore distinguish the chance which we assign to an outcome from the *real* chance of that outcome. Propensity theory is perfectly consistent with this distinction, because it allows that our measure of chance may not always accurately reflect real chance. But we can distinguish between measured chance and real chance without having to concede that the real chance of any event is either 1 or 0. The world itself may be indeterministic, so that the state of the universe at a particular time may only make it 90 per cent probable that a certain event will occur later. Are we then wrong to say that the chance of the coin's landing tails is 0.5? No, because this reflects the fact that the coin itself (considered independently of the conditions in which it is thrown) has no greater propensity to land tails than land heads.

To return to the main discussion: can we appeal to propensity theory in making sense of the idea of a godless universe being the outcome of chance? No, we cannot. For the propensity theorist, the chance of an outcome resides in the circumstances which produce the outcome. The chance of landing tails is a property of the coin, or, more accurately, of the whole situation in which the coin is thrown. But the fact that this universe was realised is not, if the atheist is right, the outcome of any *process*. Only if we accept that a creator exists can we talk of a propensity in anything to produce universes. We may imagine God contemplating, for example, a whole series of values for the speed of light and eventually coming down in favour of one. If God did this completely at random, then we could perhaps talk of its being extremely improbable that the charge on the proton should have been $1 \cdot 602 \times 10^{-19}$ coulomb. But then, if we have to introduce a creator in order to be able to talk coherently of the probability of the laws of physics being what they are, we can hardly appeal to the supposed improbability of certain combinations of those laws as an argument for God's existence.

Where does this get us? The teleological argument asks us to compare the following: (i) the probability of there being laws which permit the development of intelligent life on the hypothesis that God does exist; and (ii) the probability of there being laws which permit the development of intelligent life on the hypothesis that God does *not* exist. Probability (i) is supposed to be far greater than probability (ii), and this provides a case for theism. Now we can certainly find some kind of value for (i), at least on the propensity theory of chance, because we can talk in terms of God's propensity to produce a universe of a certain type, just as we can talk of the propensity of a fruit machine to produce the jackpot. We are not, of course, imagining God playing a game of chance ('Heads I create the universe, tails I don't'). Rather, we will reason as follows. If it is in God's nature to be benevolent, we would imagine that he would realise this benevolence by creating an object which he could love, and which, moreover, was capable of being aware of that love. God, then, has good reason to create intelligent life. The probability of there being intelligent life given God's existence, then, is high, perhaps as high as 1. But this gets us nowhere, because we cannot intelligibly assign a value to (ii). If there is no creator, then there is nothing to which we can ascribe the propensity to produce a universe. Consequently, the notion of chance is inapplicable.

In stating the principles on which the teleological argument depends, we overlooked another important principle: do not choose a hypothesis which is itself very improbable. As in the lamp case, we may be faced with competing hypotheses, all of which make the phenomenon to be explained probable. The fact that one of the hypotheses is more likely to be true than another is one reason for adopting it. For example, suppose on entering a science museum we are confronted with a perplexing sight: a tap, apparently suspended in mid-air, connected to nothing at all, and yet spouting a vertical stream of water. We are faced with competing hypotheses: (a) we are having an hallucination at just that moment; (b) there is a hollow glass tube on which the tap is fixed, and through which water is being pumped from below, so that when the water overflows from the top, it runs down the tube in such a way as to disguise its presence. Both of these hypotheses make the phenomenon to be explained probable. Indeed, the first makes it absolutely certain, because the hallucination just *is* the phenomenon. But we will almost certainly not adopt the first in preference to the second, because the chance that the first hypothesis is true is so small. So it might seem that, in order to assess whether we should adopt theism as a hypothesis, we need to know the chance of God's existing. Now, for reasons given above, we cannot make sense of such a chance, for God is supposed to be the outcome of no process whatsoever. There is nothing, therefore, which can be said to have a certain propensity to produce God. But if there is no propensity, then there is no chance of God's existing or not existing.

## THE WEAK ANTHROPIC PRINCIPLE

Despite its failure as an argument for theism, the teleological argument remains as a powerful statement of what puzzles us about the universe, and it appears, moreover, to offer an answer to that puzzlement. We may not be forced to acknowledge that we are the result of design, but we still want to have an explanation of why, for example, the fundamental constants of nature were so balanced as to allow large amounts of carbon to be available, this in turn making possible the development of life. If we are used to being able to explain things, it is very difficult simply to accept that there are certain things which are beyond explanation. But in recent years a principle has been articulated which, at least on one interpretation, offers an antidote to our puzzlement over the fact that the universe was such as to permit the development of life. Known as the *anthropic principle*, it can be stated simply, though ambiguously, as follows: 'The fundamental constants are as they are because this is a possible world in which there is life.' There are two quite different versions of the principle. One of them, which we shall examine in the next chapter, takes the mystery of the fundamental constants seriously; the other tries to defuse that puzzlement, and is called the *weak* anthropic principle. It goes as follows:

### The weak anthropic principle

What we can expect to observe must be restricted by the conditions necessary for our presence as observers.

We might call it the '"What-else-would-you-expect-to-observe?" principle'. As Descartes pointed out, we cannot doubt our own existence. So what we observe must be consistent with our own existence. So *of course* the fundamental constants will be such as to permit the development of life. Our puzzlement is groundless.

The weak anthropic principle may remind us of the trivial explanation we encountered in Chapter 3, pages 33–5. 'Why does the actual world contain a universe?' means, according to the trivial explanation, 'Why does the world in which I am located contain a universe?'. My existence is therefore a necessary condition for the question even to make sense. Similarly, the weak anthropic principle states that it is a condition of being able to ask a certain question that this world contains life. Is the weak anthropic principle therefore as suspicious as the trivial explanation? No, because the explanation offered in each case is quite different. In the case of the anthropic principle, the connection between what needs to be explained and the existence of an observer is a causal, not a logical, one. So we cannot criticise the anthropic principle in the same way as we criticised the trivial explanation: the anthropic principle does not imply the reality of other possible worlds.

However, this attempt to defuse the mystery of existence has met with some resistance. Richard Swinburne, for example, has suggested that there must be a more substantive explanation of why the fundamental constants are as they are, and in order to drive the point home he appeals to the following analogy:

Suppose that a madman kidnaps a victim and shuts him in a room with a card-shuffling machine. The machine shuffles ten packs of cards simultaneously and then draws a card from each pack and exhibits simultaneously the ten cards. The kidnapper tells the victim that he will shortly set the machine to work and it will exhibit its first draw, but that unless the draw consists of an ace of hearts from each pack, the machine will simultaneously set off an explosion which will kill the victim, in consequence of which he will not see which cards the machine drew. The machine is then set to work, and to the amazement and relief of the victim the machine exhibits an ace of hearts drawn from each pack. The victim thinks that this extra-ordinary fact needs an explanation in terms of the machine having been rigged in some way. But the kidnapper, who now reappears, casts doubt on this suggestion. 'It is hardly surprising', he says, 'that the machine draws only aces of hearts. You could not possibly see anything else. For you would not be here to see anything at all, if any other cards had been drawn.' But, of course, the victim is right and the kidnapper is wrong. There is indeed something extraordinary in need of explanation in ten aces of hearts being drawn. The fact that this peculiar order is a necessary condition of the draw being perceived at all makes what is perceived no less extraordinary and in need of explanation.

(Swinburne 1979, p. 138)

How good an analogy is this? Although Swinburne does not say so, the reason why the outcome of this fiendish experiment is so surprising is that it is extremely improbable. Given the number of combinations which the card-shuffling machine could have produced, the chance that it would produce ten aces is very small indeed – it is in fact $(1/52)^{10}$. That is why the victim naturally feels there should be some more substantive explanation than that offered by the kidnapper. But, as we are now in a position to see after the discussion of the previous section, this makes the analogy very suspicious. For the permutation of the fundamental constants is *not* the outcome of some random process, and the idea that such a permutation is very improbable is, therefore, quite inappropriate. In the language of propensity theory, whereas in the case Swinburne discusses there is an object to which one can ascribe a propensity, in the case of the fundamental constants there is no such object. No object, no propensity; no propensity, no chance.

Perhaps Swinburne is right to request a further explanation of the fundamental constants, but he cannot appeal to probabilistic considera-tions to motivate such a request. If the weak anthropic principle does not defuse the mysteries of existence, then we shall still be drawn to the explanation offered by the theist. Unless, that is, we can find a rival teleological explanation for the existence and nature of the universe which makes no reference to God. It is now time to see whether the atheist can meet this challenge.

## SUMMARY

In its traditional form in the writings of eighteenth-century theologians, the teleological argument attempted to construct an analogy between human artefacts and natural objects. Just as a watch bears the marks of its designer, so do such things as the eye. The eye has a particular purpose, that of conveying visual information. But we cannot talk of purpose here unless we can also talk of someone who designed the eye for that purpose. Hence, according to the argument, we can infer the existence of a creator.

What undermines the analogy is the discovery of a natural, non-theological explanation for phenomena like the eye, such as the theory of natural selection. However, we can construct a probabilistic version of the teleological argument which cannot be refuted by scientific developments. The probabilistic teleological argument exploits the idea that it is extremely improbable that the laws of the universe should be so balanced as to permit the development of life unless we adopt the hypothesis that these laws were fixed by a creator who desired the development of life. The argument, however, faces the same kind of objection as the one we brought against the cosmological argument in the previous chapter: it takes a certain concept out of a context in which it is obviously applicable, and applies it to a context in which that concept is not applicable. In the case of the cosmological argument, the crucial concept is that of causation; in the case of the teleological argument, it is statistical probability. Neither argument carries conviction because we can plausibly deny that the concept in question can be extended to cover extraordinary contexts.

Two theories of statistical probability were presented: the frequency theory and the propensity theory. The frequency theory equates probability with frequency in a sufficiently large population. The propensity theory equates probability with a real property in a situation to produce a particular outcome. On the basis of either theory, it makes no sense to talk of the probability of a life-sustaining universe in the absence of God.

## FURTHER READING

One of the most readable and elegant discussions of the teleological argument (and the cosmological argument) is David Hume's posthumous *Dialogues Concerning Natural Religion*, edited with an introduction by J.C.A. Gaskin, Oxford: Oxford University Press, 1993. It presents three characters: Demea, who defends the cosmological argument, Cleanthes, who presents quite convincingly the traditional version of the teleological argument, and Philo (almost certainly representing

Hume's own viewpoint), who ably dismantles both arguments. His critique of the teleological argument is particularly devastating.

For an introductory discussion of the analogical version of the argument and Hume's critique of it, see William L. Rowe, *Philosophy of Religion: An Introduction*, Belmont: Wadsworth Publishing Company, 1978, Chapter 4. See also Brian Davies, *An Introduction to the Philosophy of Religion*, Oxford: Oxford University Press, 2nd Edition, 1993, Chapter 6.

The probabilistic version of the teleological argument is presented and defended by Richard Swinburne in *The Existence of God*, Oxford: Clarendon Press, 1979, Chapter 8. This is criticised by John Mackie in Chapter 8 of *The Miracle of Theism*, Oxford: Oxford University Press, 1982.

The propensity theory of statistical probability is lucidly and persuasively defended against its rivals in D.H. Mellor's *The Matter of Chance*, Cambridge: Cambridge University Press, 1971. Mellor also exposes the misuses of probability by proponents of the teleological argument in 'God and Probability', *Religious Studies* 5 (1969), pp. 223–34.

# 5 Does the universe have a purpose?

Nothing . . . that lacks awareness tends to a goal, except under the direction of someone with awareness and with understanding; the arrow, for example, requires an archer.

St Thomas Aquinas, *Summa Theologiae*

## THE STRONG ANTHROPIC PRINCIPLE

What has the presence of human beings to do with the laws of nature? According to the anthropic principle, the latter can be explained in terms of the former. In fact, because there is more than one version of it, the anthropic principle offers *two* explanations. One version, the weak anthropic principle, states in effect that we should expect to discover laws of nature which are compatible with the existence of human observers. This was the principle introduced in the previous chapter. The other version, the strong anthropic principle, suggests something far more controversial. It goes as follows:

*The strong anthropic principle*

The universe had to be such as to permit the emergence of observers in it at some stage.

This, clearly, is a teleological principle, in that it implies that the production of life is part of the design, or purpose, of the universe, and the laws of nature being as they are is part of the realisation of that design. Whereas the weak principle is intended to defuse a mystery ('Of course the laws are compatible with human beings: what else would you expect, as a human being, to observe?'), the strong principle takes the mystery seriously ('It is indeed surprising that the laws of nature should have permitted the development of life, given the infinite variety of ways things could have turned out otherwise, so we need to appeal to purpose in order to explain what would otherwise seem a fluke.'). Now we suggested in the last chapter that the universe as a whole is not the outcome of *chance*, since the notion of chance is only applicable to a random (or apparently random) process, and neither the theist nor the atheist is going to say that the universe is the outcome of such a process. There is no universe-producing fruit machine. So we are not driven towards a hypothesis that makes it less chancy that the universe turned out to be life-supporting. We do not have to appeal to the idea of the universe being 'rigged', as it were. Nevertheless, we may still find the strong anthropic principle attractive, in so far as it answers a question we want to be answered.

The problem is whether we can make sense of the principle except in the context of theism. In giving a teleological explanation of our intentional actions ('I went to the bank in order to cash a cheque') we appeal to conscious purpose. Now, if the only intelligible use of teleology involved appeal to conscious purpose, then the strong anthropic principle would lead us towards, rather than away from, theism, for to say that the universe *had* to be such as to permit the emergence of observers would imply that someone (God?) intended that there should be observers. But just suppose for a moment that we *can* make sense of teleology without consciousness. Then the universe could have a purpose without that being the purpose of some conscious being. We would then have the beginnings of an explanation of why the universe turned out to be life-supporting which could be accepted by the atheist. So an important incentive for believing in theism, that it alone solves the mystery of the laws of nature, would have been lost.

I say that we would have the *beginnings* of an explanation, because it is still unclear why human beings should be the favoured observers. After all, conditions also favoured the emergence of sheep, and these are observers of a kind. So why should it not be appropriate to explain the laws of nature in terms of the fact that the universe had to be such as to permit the existence of sheep? Clearly, something more than species favouritism should make us put human beings at centre stage. What could this be? Here is one possible answer. First, the actions of human beings have moral properties. Second, human beings provide an object for God's benevolence. Now of course, sheep, too, provide an object for God's benevolence, but human beings provide the possibility of a fuller expression of that benevolence. In two senses, then, the existence of human beings makes possible the performance of morally good actions. So it is not the existence of human beings *per se* which explains the fact that the laws of nature are as they are, but rather the fact that human beings make possible the performance of morally good actions. This (clearly controversial) extension of the anthropic principle needs a name of its own. I propose to call it *the moral explanation*. To move from the strong anthropic principle to the moral explanation, we simply replace 'observers' with 'moral agents':

*The moral explanation:*

The laws of the universe are as they are (i.e. life-supporting) because the universe had to be such as to permit the emergence of moral agents in it at some stage.

To repeat an earlier point, if such an explanation is to be used by the atheist, we must be able to make sense of the idea that the universe has a built-in purpose, namely to produce moral agents, in the absence of a conscious being who has this purpose. We must be able to make sense of teleology without consciousness.

Well, *can* we make sense of teleology without consciousness? Aristotle certainly freely used teleology in explaining the behaviour of non-conscious organisms. For example, a plant, according to Aristotle, grows roots *in order to* gain nourishment. The plant does not intend to gain nourishment, if intending means conscious intending, and Aristotle does not suppose that the plant is conscious. Rather, human conscious purpose, in Aristotle's system, mirrors a more general purposiveness in the universe, though this may not extend beyond the realm of living things. Aristotle's world-picture, however, was gradually replaced by a mechanical picture, and few today would accept it. Nevertheless, in the last few decades biology has produced an apparently teleological principle which makes no reference to conscious purpose. Let us now consider this principle, to see what light it casts on our contemporary conception of teleology.

## TELEOLOGY AND CAUSAL REDUCTIONISM: THE SELFISH GENE HYPOTHESIS

Altruistic behaviour – the performance of acts which benefit others to the possible detriment of the agent – is not confined to human beings. (Indeed, it is not clear that humans are the most conspicuously altruistic of all species.) Here is one striking example of apparent altruism in bees. Worker bees will defend their hive against attacks from other creatures by stinging the attackers. But in protecting their hive in this way they necessarily sacrifice themselves, because the act of stinging always results in their own death. Similarly, birds may expose themselves to risk by attracting the attention of a predator away from their offspring. One explanation of this kind of behaviour, an explanation that at one time gained currency in expositions of Darwinian evolutionary theory, is that individuals perform such altruistic behaviour *in order to ensure survival of their species.* No conscious intention on the part of the animal concerned is appealed to in justification of this teleological formulation of the explanation. Rather, the behaviour is, on this account, part of their biological programming.

In a now famous book, *The Selfish Gene,* Richard Dawkins explains why biologists came to reject this view. His alternative explanation is that the fundamental unit of selection is not the species, but the gene. What is a gene? In concrete form the gene is a length of DNA (deoxyribonucleic acid) which, in conjunction with other lengths of DNA, controls the appearance of certain features in the development of an organism. The boundaries of the gene are somewhat vague. Just how much of the DNA should we count as a gene? There is no precise answer to this question, but we can still talk of genes just as we can talk of heaps. (There is no minimum size something has to be in order for it to count as a heap, but some things are correctly described as heaps and other things are not.) But considered as something which survives replication, as something which is passed on from one individual to another, the gene is a parcel of information. In what follows, 'gene' will be used in this more abstract sense.

What Dawkins calls the 'law of gene selfishness' can be given a teleological formulation, as follows: typically, the animal acts as it does in order to ensure the survival of its *genes,* even when it acts apparently altruistically. It is hardly worth remarking that the gene itself is not an object of concern to the animal (unless the animal is a geneticist), though we could certainly make sense of other animals being objects of concern for it. The animal does not act consciously for the good of the gene. Rather, the gene disposes the animal to act in such a way as to ensure its (the gene's) own survival. But, again, it is not suggested that the gene consciously intends this. Here, then, we seem to have an example of teleology without consciousness. Has Aristotle been vindicated by modern biology? In fact, Dawkins is careful to deny any suggestion of purposiveness in his account, and tries to avoid teleological formulations of the principle of gene selfishness. It is worth looking at the mechanisms which underlie this 'selfishness'.

How does the fact that the gene is the fundamental unit of selection explain apparently altruistic behaviour among animals? A successful gene is the cause of its own success. Suppose a certain gene, $x$, encourages altruistic behaviour in the individuals of a species towards their own closest relatives, as in the self-sacrificing behaviour of worker bees in protecting their hive. The beneficiaries of this behaviour also have the $x$ gene. In so far as the altruistic behaviour enables individuals with the $x$ gene to produce more individuals with the $x$ gene, the gene improves its own chances of replication. By definition, natural selection favours those genes which cause their own success above those genes whose success depends on accident. So a gene which promotes altruism towards individuals with the same genes will be favoured by natural selection, and this explains the altruistic behaviour of the bees. In general terms, the explanation of a certain pattern of behaviour according to the selfish gene hypothesis goes as follows:

1   We can expect the occurrence of any behaviour which is both caused by a certain gene and in turn causes the replicative success of that gene.
2   Behaviour $x$ is an instance of behaviour of this type

*Therefore:* We can expect behaviour type $x$.

Such an explanation can also be given of the aggressive behaviour of certain males towards rivals for the females. The gene that causes such aggression will, by increasing the chances of reproductive success on the part of the male that has this gene, increase the chances of its own replication. So aggression is replicated. And, just to emphasise the point that the selfish gene hypothesis involves no conscious purpose, we can apply this form of explanation to plants. The cactus, as Aristotle would put it, has a spongy body and thick skin in order to conserve water. The real reason, underlying this explanation of why cactuses are as they are, is that having such properties is a successful survival strategy in a dry environment. Plants with water-conserving genes have, in such an environment, a greater chance of replicating those genes than do plants without them.

In all the examples of teleological explanation we have encountered so far, there is a close link with causal explanation. If we present the facts in one way, then we have a teleological explanation. But if we present them in a different way, what we have is a causal explanation. In fact, teleological explanation can be seen as a kind of *reverse* causal explanation. With causal explanation, we explain an effect in terms of its cause. With teleological explanation, we explain a cause in terms of its effect. Table 5.1 should help to make this clear.

Now let us ask how it is that referring to the effect of a certain activity explains that activity. In the cases above, it is because the effect alludes in some indirect way to the *cause* of the activity. In other words, the teleological explanation has an underlying causal explanation. To make

*Table 5.1* Teleological explanations

| What is to be explained = the cause | Teleological relation | What provides the explanation = the effect |
|---|---|---|
| The athlete runs | for the sake of | winning the race |
| The cactus develops a thick skin | for the sake of | conserving water |
| The animal acts aggressively | for the sake of | ensuring the survival of its genes |

this clear, let us represent the activities above as effects and put them on the right hand side of the table.

Compare the right-hand column of Table 5.1 with the left-hand column of Table 5.2. There is an important connection between them. Winning the race is not just the effect of running; it is also what the athlete desires to do, and this desire is what causes him to run. Conserving water is not just the effect of having a thick skin; it is also part of the evolutionary history of the gene which is causing the cactus to grow a thick skin. It seems, then, that different kinds of explanation do not necessarily correspond to different states of affairs in the world. If we employ teleological explanations of things, we are not necessarily committing ourselves to the view that there is real purposiveness in nature. We may take the line that only causation, not purposiveness, is to be attributed to the world. The doctrine that causality is what in the world a given form of explanation depends upon can be described as a *causal reductionist* view of that form of explanation. Despite the implied teleology of its title, *The Selfish Gene* was clearly written in a spirit of

*Table 5.2* Causal explanations

| What provides the explanation = the cause | Causal relation | What is to be explained = the effect |
|---|---|---|
| The desire to win the race | causes it to be the case that | the athlete runs |
| The past success of having a thick skin in conserving water | causes it to be the case that | the cactus grows a thick skin |
| The past success of aggressive behaviour in ensuring gene replication | causes it to be the case that | the animal acts aggressively |

*Table 5.3* Incorporating the moral explanation into Table 5.1

| What is to be explained = the cause | Teleological relation | What provides the explanation = the effect |
|---|---|---|
| The laws of nature are as they are | for the sake of | producing moral agents |

causal reductionism: the connections that Dawkins is drawing attention to are, in reality, only causal connections.

What the selfish gene hypothesis illustrates is the idea that we can quite legitimately use a teleological form of explanation without having to appeal to conscious purpose. When we say that an individual acts in order to ensure the replication of its genes, we say something which can be true and illuminating, even though the individual in question may not intend its genes to be replicated. Thus we do not have to agree with Aquinas that things without consciousness tend to a goal only if their movements are controlled by someone with consciousness, for, when we see what underlies teleological explanation in such cases, the purposiveness evaporates and we are left with causal connections. We can summarise causal reductionism in these terms: there can be teleological explanation without consciousness, but there cannot be (real) teleology without consciousness.

We are now in a position to apply this understanding of teleological explanation to the moral explanation of the laws of nature. Like the selfish gene hypothesis, the moral explanation, as used by the atheist, does not appeal to *conscious* design. It does not posit a being who so designed the world that it would realise his moral purposes. Is it then possible to interpret the moral explanation in such a way as to make it consistent with causal reductionism? (I am not closing the door on a non-reductionist treatment of the moral explanation, merely postponing it until the next section.) We have no difficulty in incorporating the moral explanation into Table 5.1 (see Table 5.3), but when we come to Table 5.2, we face a difficulty (see Table 5.4).

*Table 5.4* Incorporating the moral explanation into Table 5.2

| What provides the explanation = the cause | Causal relation | What is to be explained = the effect |
|---|---|---|
| ? | causes it to be the case that | the laws of nature are as they are |

On the atheist view, *nothing* causes the laws of nature to be as they are. Some laws may be appealed to in explaining why other laws hold, but this is not to say that some laws *cause* other laws. So nothing could be placed in the left-hand column of the table. The only possible candidate for this column is 'The desire to produce moral agents'. Whose desire? Why, God's, of course. So, in spite of the fact that we can understand a form of teleological explanation which does not depend on conscious purpose, we have not yet made sense of the moral explanation outside theism. The problem, it seems, is causal reductionism. As long as we remain faithful to the view that causality is what underlies all teleological explanation, we will not allow the atheist a teleological explanation of the laws of nature. It is time, then, to look at the possibility of abandoning causal reductionism.

## TELEOLOGY WITHOUT CAUSAL REDUCTIONISM

To abandon causal reductionism is to take teleology seriously, as Aristotle did. But what in the world could it be, if not causal relations, which underlies teleological explanation? All we can say in answer to this is that, just as causal explanation has a basis in causal relations, so teleological explanation can be supposed to have a basis in *purposive* relations. We can put constraints on what is to count as genuine teleological explanation, but we can say almost nothing about the underlying basis.

Since we can only concede our ignorance on this point, the best way of defending this view of teleology is to point out that we are in no better a position with regard to causal explanation. We can put constraints on what is to count as causal explanation, we can stipulate the conditions that genuine causes must fulfil; e.g. being temporally precedent to and raising the chances of their effects, etc. But, as Hume pointed out, we can say nothing of the mechanism that underlies the causal relation. We cannot say *how* it is that causes produce their effects. To make another Humean point, even in those cases where we think we have identified the mechanism whereby A causes B, all we are in fact doing is identifying intermediate causes. To replace 'A causes B' with 'A causes B by causing C which in turn causes B' does nothing further to illuminate the nature of causal relation. The fact that we are in a similar position of ignorance in the case of teleological explanation can hardly count, therefore, as a fatal objection to such explanation.

But there are more serious problems. Do we want to say that these mysterious purposive relations are what underlie all teleological explanation? This would not be a wise step, since the teleological explanations examined in the previous section are surely much more plausibly analysed according to the causal reductionist account. The selfish gene hypothesis, according to its own proponents, works precisely because of the underlying causal relations. But, if we retain a causal reductionist account of these explanations, while providing a quite different account of the moral explanation, we cannot regard teleological explanation as a unified kind of explanation, except at a superficial level.

Finally, there is a puzzling feature of teleological explanation which the causal reductionist account can render intelligible, and which, therefore, provides a reason to stick to that account. The goal of a particular activity, such as running or growing roots, explains the activity *even in cases where the goal is never reached.* The athlete may not in fact win the race, and the plant may grow roots in barren soil. Yet how can something non-existent – an unrealised goal – explain anything? The most plausible answer is that, although the goal itself may be non-existent, it has a *causal surrogate* which does exist. In the case of the athlete, the causal surrogate is the desire to win. In the case of the plant, it is the conditions under which the plant acquired the genes which are now causing it to grow roots. Interestingly, Aristotle proposes something very like a causal surrogate for the goal of an activity:

> Things are done for something. Therefore they are by nature such as to be done for something....
>
> The point is most obvious if you look at those animals other than men, which make things not by art, and without carrying out inquiries or deliberation. Spiders, ants, and the like have led people to wonder how they accomplish what they do, if not by mind. Descend a little further, and you will find things coming to be which conduce to an end even in plants, for instance leaves for the protection of fruit. If, then, the swallow's act in making its nest is both due to nature and for something, and the spider's in making its web, and the plant's in producing leaves for its fruit, and roots not up but down for nourishment, plainly this sort of cause is present in things...
>
> (Aristotle, *Physics*, Book II, Chapter 8, 199a10–30.
> Charlton (1970), pp. 40–1.)

Although the end, or goal, of the activity may never be realised, in the sense that the plant may fail to gain nourishment, there is a sense in which the end is present *in the plant.* Even if we reject causal reductionism, we will have to allow some kind of surrogate for an unrealised goal, and once we do this, it is almost impossible not to think of it as some kind of *causal* surrogate.

The moral explanation of the laws of nature, then, remains highly problematic. It seems that it would be better for the atheist to give up the attempt to explain why the laws of the universe are life-favouring, rather than introduce something so metaphysically suspect. It looks as if the theist has won this particular skirmish. But we need to examine more closely the idea that a creator can introduce purpose into the world. If human existence has a point, that of realising God's moral purposes, then there must be something special about God. For we would not think that there was something necessarily valuable about a life which realised someone else's purposes unless we thought those purposes were intrinsically admirable. What is special about God, for the theist, is that morality is *based* on God: what is right is defined in terms of God's wishes. But this idea provides the atheist with a means of attack, as we shall now see.

## SUMMARY

The strong anthropic principle ascribes a purpose to the universe: the laws of nature are life-favouring because the universe had to be such as to permit the emergence of intelligent observers at some stage. To the question, 'Why should the observers be human?', it might be answered that human observers are capable of moral actions. This gives us a version of the anthropic principle that we labelled *the moral explanation*: the laws of nature are life-favouring because the universe had to be such as to permit the emergence of moral agents at some stage.

The theist can make perfect sense of the moral explanation by ascribing the ultimate purpose to God. The question is whether the atheist can make sense of it. If he can, then the atheist has a teleological, purposive, explanation of the universe to rival the theist's. For this to be possible, we have to allow that teleological explanation is appropriate even when conscious purposes are not present.

One such teleological explanation is the selfish gene hypothesis, which states that living things behave as they do in order to ensure the survival of their genes. However, scrutiny of the hypothesis revealed that it was based on causal reductionism, the view that teleological explanation depends only on the existence of causes. It was argued that causal reductionism is the most plausible account of teleological explanation. Most importantly, it shows how we can explain things by their goals even when those goals are not realised. However, causal reductionism is incompatible with an atheist interpretation of teleological explanation. The theist's use of the moral explanation, in contrast, seems entirely consistent with causal reductionism, since God's design is encoded in his intentions which themselves cause the universe to exist. The limits of this kind of explanation, however, were discussed in Chapter 3.

## FURTHER READING

An introductory presentation of the weak and strong anthropic principles is provided in Chapter 5 of P.C.W. Davies' *The Accidental Universe*, Cambridge: Cambridge University Press, 1982. See also John Leslie's *Universes*, New York: Routledge, 1989.

A form of moral explanation, under the name of 'extreme axiarchism', is developed and defended at length in John Leslie's *Value and Existence*, Oxford: Blackwell, 1979. See also his article 'Efforts to explain all existence', in *Mind* 87 (1978), pp. 181–94. Leslie's views are neatly summarised, though quickly dismissed, by John Mackie in Chapter 13 of *The Miracle of Theism*, Oxford: Oxford University Press, 1982.

Richard Dawkins's now famous presentation of natural selection is to be found in *The Selfish Gene*, 2nd Edition, Oxford: Oxford University Press, 1989.

For an accessible introduction to Aristotle's theory of explanation, including his conception of teleological explanation, see Jonathan Lear, *Aristotle: The Desire to Understand*, Cambridge: Cambridge University Press, 1988, Chapter 2.

# Part II
# Moral arguments for atheism

# 6 Are God and ethics inseparable or incompatible?

> They that deny a God destroy a man's nobility, for certainly Man is of kin to the beasts by his body; and if he be not of kin to God by his spirit, he is a base and ignoble creature.
>
> Francis Bacon, *Of Atheism*

## PLATO'S DILEMMA

Consider the following doctrines:

(a) God is good.
(b) God wills us to do what is good.
(c) God is the basis of ethics.

The first and second of these are held true in Christian, Judaic and Islamic thought. They are not, however, essential to the idea of a creator of the universe. There could be a transcendent creator of the universe who has no moral attributes, or who is indifferent to our moral state. But, in this chapter, we shall consider those varieties of theism which argue for a tight connection between God and morality. This takes us to doctrine (c). What it asserts is that a proper understanding of the nature of morality must make reference to God, an idea that, in one form or other, has played a crucial role in theistic thought. Expressed like this, however, the idea is somewhat vague, and open to more than one interpretation. Here is one, not very plausible, interpretation: morally correct behaviour depends on belief in God. If this implies, as it seems to, that atheists are liable to behave badly, then we can reject it quite quickly. Atheists may have exactly the same views about what counts as good and bad, and may behave just as well, or as badly, as theists. A more interesting interpretation of (c) goes as follows: in deciding what is right, the theist may make use of some religious image. For example, the Christians may take Jesus as the model on which to base their idea of right conduct. In this sense, faith informs moral conduct.

However, in this chapter, I want to pursue a quite different, and more metaphysical, interpretation of (c), namely the idea that the existence of God explains the existence of moral values. The fact that certain acts are good or bad depends in some way on God and his properties. Some theists have appealed to this explanatory role in arguing for the existence of God. The argument, known as the 'moral argument' for God, goes roughly like this:

*The moral argument*

1  There are moral values.
2  The existence of these values depends on the existence and nature of God.

*Therefore:* God exists.

Premise (2), note, is one way of rephrasing doctrine (c).

It will be helpful at this point to make a distinction between *ethics* (or 'first-order' ethics), and *meta-ethics* (or 'second-order' ethics). Ethics is concerned with such questions as what the best kind of life would be, or what I ought to do and which rules to adopt by which I could decide what I ought to do. Meta-ethics, in contrast, is concerned with the status of ethical judgements. 'Is theft wrong?' is an ethical question. 'Are there objective moral values?' is a meta-ethical question. Some theists believe that there is an important connection between God and ethics, in that in deciding what to do I must make appeal to God. What in contrast we are now concerned with is the idea that there is an important connection between God and *meta*-ethics, in that a proper understanding of what is involved in ethical judgements must involve appeal to God.

The aim of this chapter is not so much to undermine the moral argument for God's existence, though this will be one result of the discussion, but rather to cast doubt on the idea that the existence of moral values depends on God. The problem with doctrine (c), given this interpretation of it, is that it makes difficulties for our understanding of (a) and (b) – a problem first noted by Plato.

In his dialogue the *Euthyphro*, which is concerned with the nature of piety, Plato presents us with the following question: 'How are we to understand the idea that God wills us to do what is good?' There are two answers we could give to this question:

A  God wills us to do what is good because certain acts *are* good, and he wishes such actions to be performed.
B  An act is good only because God wills it.

It seems that, whichever way we answer the question, we get an unhappy result – or at least an unhappy result for the theist. Suppose we choose answer (A): God wills what is good because, independently of his will, it *is* good. It seems to follow from this that moral values exist independently of God. That is, even if God had not existed, there would still have been moral values, so the basis of ethics has nothing to do with theism. This goes against the theist assertion that ethics is informed by the fact that God exists, in that we cannot divorce questions concerning what is right from questions concerning God's design for us. If, on the other hand, we opt for answer (B), and say that something is good by virtue of the fact that God wills it, then the assertion that God wills us to perform good acts just reduces to the unenlightening assertion that God wills us to do what he wills us to do. Of the three doctrines that we began this section with, then, (b) appears to conflict with (c), under its metaphysical interpretation. There is also an apparent conflict between (a) and (c), for, if ascribing goodness to something just means that God wills it, then the assertion that God is good becomes the curious and morally empty assertion that God wills that he be as he is. This can hardly be represented as one of the foundation stones of the religious life. This problem is neatly captured by Bertrand Russell in his essay 'Why I am not a Christian':

> If you are going to say, as theologians do, that God is good, you must then say that right and wrong have some meaning which is independent of God's fiat, because God's fiats are good and not bad independently of the mere fact that he made them. If you are going to say that, you will then have to say that it is not only through God that right and wrong came into being, but that they are in their essence logically anterior to God.
>
> (Russell 1957, p. 19)

This amounts to more than just a criticism of the moral argument for God (which was Russell's target at that point in his essay), for we can present these reflections in a more structured way to provide an argument against theism on the ground that it contains an inconsistency. It cannot be true both that the existence of moral values depends on God *and* that the statement 'God is good' makes a morally significant assertion. Consequently, theism is false, because it is incoherent. Making the moves absolutely explicit, we can construct an argument for atheism which exploits a version of premise (2) of the moral argument for God. We can call it the 'meta-ethical argument for atheism':

*The meta-ethical argument for atheism*

1   If theism is true then 'God is good' is morally significant.

2  If theism is true then God plays an explanatory role in ethics.
3  If 'God is good' is morally significant, then moral goodness must be independent of God.
4  If God plays an explanatory role in ethics, moral goodness cannot be independent of God.

*Therefore:* Theism is false.

How exactly is the conclusion reached? Taking it more slowly, (1) and (3) together imply (5):

5  If theism is true then moral goodness must be independent of God.

However, (2) and (4) together imply (6):

6  If theism is true then moral goodness cannot be independent of God.

Putting (5) and (6) together, we obtain:

7  If theism is true then moral goodness both is, and is not, independent of God.

Theism, in other words, is self-contradictory and hence false.

We can construct an exactly parallel argument, substituting 'God wills us to do what is good' for 'God is good'. By doing this, we capture the challenge to theism posed by Plato's dilemma.

Now, in order to reach the conclusion of the meta-ethical argument, we have had to ascribe to the theist a particular philosophical doctrine, namely that the existence of moral value is explained in some way by the existence and properties of God. Not all theists will necessarily assent to this meta-ethical assertion. But for the more philosophically inclined theists, this is an important aspect of God. God, for them, explains the existence of many things, and, since God is also a moral being, it is entirely natural to suppose that moral value somehow resides in God. So theists have a reason to defend premise (2) of the meta-ethical argument. What they must do, then, is to resist its apparent consequences. To do this, they must attack the argument at some point. The most contro-versial premise of the argument, I suggest, is (3). To see whether or not it is true, we need to examine the concept of goodness.

## DESCRIPTIVE VERSUS PRESCRIPTIVE MORALITY

Consider once again Plato's question: 'Does God will us to do what is good because, independently of him, it *is* good, or is it that what is good is so only because he wills it?' The assumption here is that we must choose one or the other, not both, and at first sight it does indeed seem that we cannot say 'yes' in response to both of these questions. However, the word 'good' can be defined in more than one way, and the possibility arises that, in one sense of 'good', acts are good *independently* of God's willing us to do them, and that, in another sense of 'good', acts are good *because* he wills them. John Mackie has suggested that, by making a distinction between different senses of 'good', the theist can escape Plato's dilemma (though not other snares, according to Mackie, who is no apologist for theism). If this is so, then the theist may also be able to escape the meta-ethical argument. So let us look at the distinction in question.

We can distinguish between the *descriptive* and the *prescriptive* elements in morality. It is the case that $x$ is a good thing to do for $y$, in a purely descriptive sense, if $x$ benefits $y$ in some way: it enables $y$ to live a happy life, say, or it contributes to the stability of the society in which $y$ lives. 'Good' in this descriptive sense attaches to a wide variety of actions. It is a good thing for $y$ to eat, to dress according to the weather, to communicate, to refrain from ending the lives of a large number of people, etc. Morally good actions constitute a subset of this class. But, in addition to this descriptive sense of 'good', there is a sense which carries an implication of requirement: there are certain things that one ought to do. To recognise that $x$ is good in the prescriptive sense is to recognise an obligation to do it. Of course, we can appropriately talk of 'ought' even if we are using 'good' in a merely descriptive sense: one ought to eat, to remain upright when walking, and so on. But the 'ought' here is only hypothetical, or conditional upon some purpose. One ought to eat *if* one wants to stay alive, one ought to act on one's desires *if* one wants them to be satisfied. In contrast, the prescriptive sense of 'good' carries with it an unconditional 'ought': one ought to refrain from killing, full stop, not merely if one wants to avoid censure. These two senses of 'good' are not necessarily in opposition to each other, though it would be possible to maintain that only the descriptive sense of 'ought' is legitimate, and that therefore the only kind of obligation there is is a conditional one. On this view, one ought to behave morally only if one wants to bring about a certain end, such as the greatest happiness of the greatest number, or the leading of a fulfilling life. So, in making the distinction, *and* holding that there are actions which are good in a prescriptive sense, we are not just defining words, we are assenting to a certain conception of morality. What this conception is will emerge as we proceed, but, for the time being, we will consider the suggestion that the distinction undermines Plato's dilemma.

Something can be descriptively good, i.e. in our best interests, whether or not God wills it, and so in this sense is good independently of God's will. Of course, if theism is right, even descriptive goodness is not entirely independent of God, since he created things in such a way that doing certain things would be good for us, but that God wills us to do what, as a matter of fact, is good for us does not reduce to the triviality that he wills us to do what he wills us to do. He wills us to do what is descriptively good (i.e. good for us) because he is benevolent: he wants us to do what will enable us to live in harmony with others compatibly with pursuing the goal of self-fulfilment. So what is descriptively good is independent of God's will, in the sense that we do not have to refer to God in defining it, although it may be that God is the causal explanation of why, as a matter of fact, certain things are good for us. However, we can say quite consistently with this that the fact that something is prescriptively good is not independent of, but constituted by, God's will. The additional element of requirement that attaches to morally good actions is provided by God's *requiring* us to do those things. So he wills us to do what is descriptively good, such as to eat and to refrain from killing each other, but, in addition, places on us an unconditional requirement to perform certain of these descriptively good actions. He does not require us to eat, but he does require us to refrain from killing. The fact that there is a distinctive group of descriptively good actions which are morally valuable does depend directly on God's will. The good, $x$, is prescriptively good because God requires it, not merely because he wills it. The theist can then present this as God's crucial explanatory role in ethics.

Consider now the assertion that 'God is good'. The meta-ethical argument presents us, in effect, with the following dilemma: either 'God is good' is morally insignificant, or moral goodness is independent of God. Can we employ the descriptive/prescriptive distinction to avoid both horns of this dilemma? Mackie's suggestion is that, when we attribute goodness to God, this is to be understood in purely descriptive terms, that God is disposed to do things which are good for us. It should not be taken as meaning that God does what he is required to do, for, since only God can place this requirement on any agent, it would mean that God requires himself to do what he does, and this has no moral content to it whatsoever. So both Plato's dilemma and the meta-ethical argument can be seen as conflating two distinct senses of 'good'.

A way out of Plato's dilemma and the meta-ethical argument has been provided for the theist. But is it the right way out for the theist to take? I suggest not. The descriptive sense of 'good' is surely too weak to capture the theist's conception. If the only coherent meaning we can ascribe to 'God is good' is that he is disposed to do good things for us, then he is good only in a conditional sense. If we value certain things, then God is good. If we do not, then he is not. No theist is likely to settle for such a weak reading of 'God is good'.

So far we have considered (a) and (c) of the theist's doctrines as if they were quite independent propositions. But if, instead, we think of them as being closely related, another way of disarming the meta-ethical argument suggests itself. When we say 'God is good', part of what we mean, no doubt, is that God is at least analogous to a morally good member of the human race. That is, God has some properties that we would consider good in a human. For example, just as good parents (in the sense of morally good, not just effective, parents) would take care of their children, so God takes care of his creation. But this cannot exhaust the goodness of God, for there are few analogies we can draw between ourselves and a divine being. What else is implied in the statement that God is good may be that, unlike humans, God is a source of moral value. That is, God's goodness in part consists of the fact that he is the basis of ethics. Since it is not trivial that God plays such a role, it cannot be trivial that God is good; in fact it is highly morally significant, because it points to the source of moral obligation. What effect do these considerations have on the meta-ethical argument? They appear to undermine premise (3):

3  If 'God is good' is morally significant, then moral goodness must be independent of God.

We can now see that this need not be true at all. The theist can, surely, hold that 'God is good' is morally significant *because* it identifies the source of moral obligation, which implies that moral goodness is not independent of God. So (3) should be replaced with:

3*  If 'God is good' is morally significant then moral goodness is *not* independent of God.

But, of course, this completely blocks the meta-ethical argument.

## MORAL REALISM AND MORAL SUBJECTIVISM

The atheist has another line of attack, however. The attempt to show that theism is internally inconsistent when it comes to facts about morality may have failed, but the atheist can instead attempt to show that the most plausible theory concerning the basis of ethics leaves no room for God to play any significant role in the explanation of moral value.

Let us begin by considering a problem to which ethics should have an answer. It is agreed by everybody that moral properties go hand-in-hand with certain non-moral, or natural, properties. Suppose that I freely and deliberately deprive someone of their livelihood – for example, by burning down the local tea shop. I do this simply because I want to, not because there is any conflict between the owners' interests and mine – for example, because I disapprove of tea-drinking, or because I wish to avenge some harm they have done me. That this act of mine is wrong there can be little doubt. Suppose now that everything that one could say about this act, apart from its being morally wrong, could also truly be said about another act, done by someone else. Then, if the first act is wrong, so is the second. The general principle on which this rests is that moral properties (such as being wrong) *supervene* on certain natural properties (such as causing gratuitous injury): i.e. that if two acts share all the relevant natural properties, they also share the same moral properties. This is not to say that moral properties are nothing but natural properties, merely that there is a systematic correlation between them. Now here is the problem: what makes it the case that certain moral properties supervene on certain natural properties? Why should there be this invariable connection?

This problem is particularly acute for the moral realist. *Moral realism* holds that it is an objective, mind-independent fact that an act, defined according to its natural properties, has the moral value that it does. Consider suicide. To define it as the intentional taking of one's own life is to define it in a morally neutral way, according to its natural properties. Now, suppose one thinks that such an act is wrong. The problem is then to *explain* why any act with these natural properties is wrong. Theism has an answer to this question: it is because of God that acts with certain natural properties also have a certain moral property. God condemns acts with natural properties $x$, $y$ and $z$, and that is what makes such acts wrong. But now another problem arises: how do we become aware that certain acts have the moral properties they do? Do we have some special faculty of moral intuition which makes 'visible', as it were, these moral properties? Does God reveal to us, every time we witness an act, his approval or condemnation of it? In contrast to the strangeness of these ideas is a natural account of moral properties which the atheist can offer, and which answers both the problem of moral knowledge and the problem of the relationship between moral and natural properties in one step. If we accept this natural account, then there is little room for God in ethics.

The account the atheist can give goes as follows. Moral properties are a reflection of our own feelings of approval or revulsion. These feelings may to some extent be innate, but no doubt others are socially conditioned. Leaving that issue on one side for the moment, the reason why moral properties supervene on natural properties is that acts with certain natural properties (e.g. the deliberate taking of human life) tend to cause in us feelings of revulsion, pity, etc., and thus lead us to condemn the act. Saying 'this is wrong' is simply an expression of that feeling, so moral properties are not properties which acts have in addition to their natural properties, and whose connection with natural properties is therefore mysterious. Once we accept this, we can see that there is no problem about moral knowledge. We 'know' that acts with certain natural properties are wrong simply because they cause certain feelings within us. This view is called *moral subjectivism*.

There are a number of variations on this central idea. The atheist could draw an analogy between moral properties and colours. The colour of an object supervenes on certain facts about its surface structure, in particular on facts about the way in which the (in themselves colourless) atoms are arranged. We might initially be puzzled by this: why should two things identical in terms of the micro-structure of their surfaces have identical colours, when viewed under the same conditions? The accepted answer, of course, is that the arrangement of atoms determines which wavelengths of light hitting the surface are absorbed and which are reflected. This, in turn, causes us to have certain sensations when the reflected light hits our retinas, and in response we attribute a certain colour to the object. This does not mean that colours are just 'in the head': they are genuine properties of the object, but properties of a certain kind, namely dispositions of the object to affect us in certain ways. Exploiting this analogy, the atheist could say that the moral properties of acts were genuine properties of the acts themselves: dispositions that those acts had to affect us in certain ways, to evoke admiration or anger. Alternatively, the atheist could say that moral properties *were* just in the head, and so mind-dependent, and that any moral judgement, such as 'this is wrong', was equivalent in meaning to 'I disapprove of that'. Such a theory of moral judgements is known as 'emotivism'. We need not get into the issue over whether emotivism is the correct account of moral values. The atheist does not need to commit himself to a particular theory about what people really mean when they give utterance to moral judgements. The important point is that he can give an account of what the connection is between the natural properties of an act and the moral property we ascribe to that act, an account which does not make our moral knowledge entirely puzzling.

What role does God have to play in all this? None whatsoever, it seems: moral knowledge and supervenience can apparently be explained without reference to God. However, the account is not actually incompatible with God's playing some explanatory role in ethics, though the role is less significant perhaps than the one originally envisaged. We can make room for God in the atheist's account by assigning to God the job of so constructing us that we respond emotionally in the way we do to certain natural properties of acts. God, as we might put it, is responsible for our moral psychology. This is a somewhat less central role than the one we canvassed at the end of the previous section, that the wrongness of an act was constituted by God's disapproval, but it does show that theism can be made consistent with moral subjectivism. However, alternative and more plausible accounts are available of how we come to respond as we do to the natural properties of acts. Our moral psychology may be a result of biological or social evolution: societies in which certain emotional responses are reinforced may be more likely to survive than other societies, and that is why these responses have become the norm. Again, God is not pushed out altogether, for the theist can point out that the mechanisms of biological and social evolution themselves call for explanation, and God is needed to fix the laws as they are. All this will eventually have repercussions in the development of moral beliefs, but now God is being placed at some distance from the facts which constitute moral values. To retain the connection between God's goodness and the facts which constitute moral goodness, the theist must insist that God does have a moral design for the world, and that this design is reflected in the laws that he makes. He does not directly implant moral notions into people's minds. We must be careful, however, not to reintroduce the notion that God desires the best for us *because* God is good, for then we are faced with Plato's dilemma all over again.

It seems that we can square theism with different accounts of the relation between moral and natural properties, of how we can have moral knowledge, and of how we come to have the moral psychology that we do, even though we have had to present (a) as a consequence of (c), rather than a doctrine with significance in its own right. But there are two further features of our conception of morality which are somewhat harder to square with theism, and to those we now turn.

## PLURALISM AND AUTONOMY

Many of us live in societies which are pluralist in their political, social, religious and moral outlook: we live side by side with people who have radically different views, and in a genuinely pluralist society the coexistence of these different views is a peaceful one. Indeed, we may not only tolerate pluralism, we may actually welcome it and regard debate between rival ideologies as beneficial to all sides. Even where there is no common ground upon which rival parties can discuss the relative merits of their views, as is the case typically with different religions, it is still possible to see the presence of incommensurable views as an enrichment of one's culture. If we take this view, then we are likely to view the breakdown of understanding and tolerance between different ideologies as deeply unfortunate. Now, if it is possible for a pluralist society to be a stable one, as many people believe, then it is hard to see such a society as simply an intermediate stage in the development of a society with a single ideological outlook. Yet, if God has a moral design for the world, and so constructs the world that his ideal will eventually be realised, then a pluralist society can at best be seen as a stage on the way to this goal, and not a desirable end in itself. Further, if God is responsible for our moral psychology, or for the conditions which determine our moral psychology, then many of us, it seems, have developed the wrong moral responses to the natural properties of acts: we condemn as wrong some things which are either right or of no moral significance, and acquiesce in some things which are wrong. Is the mechanism by which we develop our moral views then imperfect? Surely not, or else the universe would simply be a bungled experiment. Can religion help us to form the correct view? Not if a number of equally compelling, but incompatible, religions are on offer.

When we reflect that the coexistence of different moral values within a society may be preferable to an ideologically monolithic one, moral relativism becomes a plausible position. According to relativism, there are no absolute moral truths, which are the same from one context to another, but, rather, there is a given moral judgement that will only be true relative to a particular context, where 'context' means a group of people sharing an outlook and culture. That is to say, moral values are in part constituted by moral attitudes, which will vary from context to context. If relativism is correct, then the theist faces an uncomfortable choice: either God has properties which are good with respect to one society but not with respect to another, or God is morally neutral. Now pluralism does not entail relativism, but they are natural partners.

I want, finally, to consider whether there is room for God to play another explanatory role in ethics, namely the role of providing a rationale for genuinely moral actions.

Why should I refrain from harming others? 'Because God commands it.' What kind of rationale for action is this? If I do something because I believe that God commands it, then I must believe that I should obey God. But here there is a danger of regress: I should obey God because I should obey an infinitely wise, benevolent being, and I should obey an infinitely wise, benevolent being because I should ... and so on. To avoid the regress, the theist must justify obedience to God, not by appealing to some other set of obligations, but by showing how God could have a special moral authority. The authority must be special because, in general, if I do something only because someone else requires it, and not because of the features of the act itself, then I am not behaving morally. I may appear to be behaving morally, for example if I dash into a burning house to save someone lying unconscious on the first floor. But if I turn out to have done this simply because I was told to, and I would have been just as happy to recite 'Twas brillig, and the slithy toves did gyre and gimble in the wabe' if I had been told to do that instead, then my action is not moral. So why should acting in response to *God's* commands make my action a moral one?

One answer is that acting in response to God's commands is acting morally because God defines what is good: *x* is good if and only if God commands it. So to judge that *x* is good is, *ipso facto*, to judge that God commands *x*. This is why obedience to God is a special case: it imparts a moral aspect to my actions that obedience to no other authority could impart. So I do act because of the intrinsic worth of the act. However, there is still reason to think that performing an act because one believes that God commands it gets in the way, as it were, of acting morally.

Compare these two desires: the desire to subordinate oneself utterly to the wishes of some authority, so that everything one does is eventually an unconscious reflection of those wishes; and the desire that one's behaviour should reflect one's own ideals, to act because one thinks it is right, independently of the will of any other individual. Which is the better ideal, as far as our moral development is concerned? The atheist insists that the second desire is the better one. For the atheist the moral ideal is *autonomy*, or self-government. The truly moral agent is one who wishes to be his own master, not the instrument of some other power, and not to trust the deliverances of some supposed authority, but to work out for themselves the rightness of certain kinds of behaviour. But, if we value autonomy, then we distance God from morality: what God wants will not feature essentially in our deliberations. If it does, we will still want to ask whether God's wishes reflect what we believe is right. The danger of a morality which subordinates the agent's wishes and beliefs to those of an authority is that it can be based on fear of the consequences of transgression. But a morality based on fear is no morality at all.

To value moral autonomy is not necessarily to subscribe to some controversial meta-ethical theory. It is not, for example, to embrace moral scepticism and deny, or doubt, the existence of moral values. It is more likely to go together with an honest attempt to work out moral values. The autonomous agent is no more likely to be amoral than an unquestioning believer. Nor does autonomy necessarily lead one to moral relativism, the view that moral values vary from context to context. The autonomous agent may well believe in the existence of objective moral values. Autonomy would then consist in working out what those values are.

We have not shown that autonomy is inconsistent with theism. After all, God may want us to be free agents, working out our own reasons for doing things and doing them because we want to and because we see them as having intrinsic worth, just as parents want their children ultimately to be self-governing. But if this is God's design for the world, then the consequence is that morality need not make essential reference to God. So this is one more reason to suppose theism to be explanatorily redundant.

In the next chapter, we shall see whether theists can turn moral autonomy to their own advantage in meeting what is arguably the most serious problem for theism: the problem of evil.

## SUMMARY

The idea that the existence of moral values depends in some way on God creates difficulties both for the doctrine that God is good and for the doctrine that he wills us to do what is good. The problem is this: we can, apparently, only make sense of these doctrines if we think of goodness as being defined independently of God. But if it is so defined, then God does not, after all, explain the existence of moral values. Thus, theism can be presented as containing an inconsistency. This we called the 'meta-ethical argument' for atheism. It is, however, possible to avoid the contradiction if we argue that God is good precisely because his existence explains the existence of moral value. The goodness of God is thus radically unlike the goodness of ordinary moral agents.

This raises a further problem, however. If God is the basis of moral values, then such values must be objective, and we are, therefore, faced with the following questions: (1) How do we come to be aware of these moral values, if they exist entirely independently of us? (2) Why do moral facts supervene on natural facts? (3) How can the existence of objective moral values be reconciled with the existence of different conceptions of what is right? These difficulties are not faced by the atheist, who can provide the following account of moral knowledge: acts with certain natural properties tend to cause in us feelings of revulsion which, in turn, lead us to describe those acts as wrong. So the 'wrongness' of an act is simply the disposition of the act to cause a feeling of revulsion in us. But our reactions are not entirely biologically programmed: they are, in addition, influenced by our culture, hence the variety of moral systems.

There is, however, more than one way in which God could play an explanatory role in ethics. If we think of his role in these terms, that an act is good only by virtue of the fact that God wills it, then we trivialise the assertion that God wills us to do what is good. However, his role might be a rather more indirect one. The existence of God is quite compatible with the atheist's account of our moral psychology, for God may have caused us to react in the ways that we do to acts with certain natural properties. However, it is much harder to reconcile theism both with the existence of morally pluralistic cultures, and with the view that such cultures are, in a sense, preferable to morally homogeneous cultures.

The final problem we discussed was that of autonomy: if the best kind of moral agent is autonomous, i.e. self-governing, then we should not appeal to the will of God as a motivation for performing the right action. Autonomous morality is, by definition, independent of God, so, in one sense, God is not required as a basis of ethics.

**FURTHER READING**

The dilemma which begins this chapter is based on the discussion in Plato's *Euthyphro*, which is most easily available in *Plato, The Last Days of Socrates*, eds. Hugh Tredennick and Harold Tarrant, Harmondsworth: Penguin, 1993. It is discussed in John Mackie, *Ethics: Inventing Right and Wrong*, Harmondsworth: Penguin, 1977, Chapter 10. The first chapter of this book contains an excellent introduction to meta-ethics, explaining the distinction between moral objectivism and moral subjectivism and presenting succinctly and lucidly the arguments for subjectivism. His account of the relation between moral and natural properties, which we presented above (see pages 80–1), owes something to David Hume: see the *Enquiry Concerning the Principles of Morals*, edited by L.A. Selby-Bigge, 3rd Edition revised by P.H. Nidditch, Oxford: Clarendon Press, 1975.

For a discussion of the variety of connections which have been drawn between morality and religion, see Chapter 9 of Brian Davies, *An Introduction to the Philosophy of Religion*, 2nd Edition, Oxford: Oxford University Press, 1993. See also the readings in Paul Helm (ed.), *Divine Commands and Morality*, Oxford: Oxford University Press, 1981, especially the Introduction and the essay by William Frankena, 'Is Morality Logically Dependent on Religion?'.

The significance of moral pluralism for theism is highlighted in Don Cupitt's *The Leap of Reason*, London: SCM Press, 1976; and his *Taking Leave of God*, London: SCM Press, 1980, an important statement of a new religious outlook, emphasises the role of autonomy in bringing about the collapse of traditional theism.

# 7 Is there a problem of evil?

Then the Lord answered Job out of the whirlwind and said,
Who is this that darkeneth counsel by words without knowledge? . . .
Where wast thou when I laid the foundations of the earth? declare,
if thou hast understanding.

*The Book of Job*

## DISASTER, DEPRAVITY, DEITY AND DESIGN

It is an indisputable fact that the history of the world contains some of the most appalling suffering imaginable, suffering that is either the result of natural disaster, such as earthquakes, volcanic eruptions, disease and famine, or the result of human actions, such as wars, ecological disasters and religious persecution. Does this present a problem for theism? Certainly there is a case to answer if we believe in a deity who is all-knowing, all-powerful and perfectly good. If he is all-knowing, he will be aware of suffering; if he is all-powerful, he will be able to prevent suffering; and if he is perfectly good, he will desire to prevent suffering. But, clearly, he does not prevent suffering, so either there is no such deity, or, if there is, he is not all-knowing, all-powerful *and* perfectly good, though he may be one or two of these.

That is the classic version of the most powerful and convincing argument for atheism, the 'problem of evil'. It is a far more direct challenge to the existence of God than the still significant considerations of the previous chapters. The theist may admit that philosophical arguments for the existence of God fail, that theism does not provide an adequate explanation of the universe, and that God does not provide a basis for ethics. But the fact of suffering faces theists with a truth that is both undeniable and apparently incompatible with their belief.

Various strategies are open to theists, however. They may deny that even a perfectly good God would desire to eliminate *all* suffering. Indeed, suffering may be part of the divine design, in so far as suffering is an essential consequence of the realisation of some greater good. The theist who takes this line of justifying the existence of suffering faces the challenge of explaining the *amount* of suffering in the world. If we grant that some suffering may be necessary for the realisation of some divine goal, there is still the objection that there is simply too much suffering in the world for this to be an adequate explanation. Some of the worst suffering, in other words, seems entirely gratuitous.

Another strategy is simply to refuse to attempt a justification of suffering, on the grounds that God's mind is inscrutable. We cannot know God's purposes, so we should not expect to be able to understand why God permits the presence of terrible suffering in his creation. We must simply trust that there is a reason for it which our limited minds are not capable of grasping. This is, essentially, God's advice to Job when, after a series of disasters, Job dares to ask why this apparently unwarranted suffering has been visited upon a virtuous man. Later, in pages 99–102, we shall examine the question of whether this strategy can be consistently pursued.

There is a more extreme strategy which, though not favoured by any theist, is worth mentioning, and that is to *deny* the supposedly undeniable fact of suffering. We can be deluded about many things; why not about this, too? The history of philosophy is full of arguments to the effect that some fundamental aspect of our experience is illusory. Change, space and time, physical objects, free will: the reality of each of these has been denied at some time or other. We can take this further and put ourselves in the position imagined by Descartes, in which all aspects of our experience are illusory and that we only see things as we do because we are being deluded by some powerful demon, or that we are in fact merely brains kept alive in a laboratory and stimulated by some complex machine manipulated by a crazed scientist whose only amusement is to delude us into thinking that we are embodied agents. If we cannot absolutely rule out these bizarre possibilities, then it seems we know absolutely nothing at all. Any belief is open to question. How, then, can we be confident that there is such a thing as suffering? It is not surprising that no theist wants to take this sceptical line, for it undermines the theist's position. If we can doubt all things, including suffering, then we can doubt the existence of God, or the cogency of any argument for the existence of God. What is important about the problem of evil is that the presence of suffering is far more certain than the existence of God, so if there is any incompatibility here it is the theistic hypothesis which must be rejected. In any case, one thing that we cannot possibly doubt is the existence of our own suffering. If it seems to us that we are in pain, or mental anguish, then we are indeed suffering, even if we are just brains in a laboratory. The crazed scientist cannot *delude* us into thinking that we are suffering, because suffering is part of the experience itself. If he makes us think we suffer, then we really do suffer, even though we may be mistaken about the cause of that suffering. The theist cannot but admit the reality of suffering.

It is important to separate natural disasters, as a cause of suffering, from human causes, since it seems appropriate for the theist to approach them in different ways. Consider first natural disasters. (Ecological disasters such as the erosion of the ozone layer are not 'natural', in the sense we are concerned with here, since they are to be attributed to human interference with the course of nature.) They must be, at least indirectly, caused by God, so they must be made sense of in terms of the divine plan: they must serve some purpose. One answer is that natural disasters play an important role in the evolution of conscious, intelligent, and therefore moral, beings. Without at least one such disaster, after all, the earth might still be ruled by giant reptiles. Natural disasters, with their concomitant suffering, are just an unfortunate side-effect in the development of a world capable of sustaining intelligent life.

Of greater concern to writers on the topic of evil is the suffering deliberately caused by the moral depravity of human beings. This problem is at once less serious and more serious than the case of natural disasters. It is less serious because the fact that human beings are the (immediate) cause of suffering can be exploited by the theist to distance God from evil. God is not responsible for the suffering inflicted by the free actions of human beings, it is suggested. But why then did God create free human agents? Because there would simply have been no point, for God, in creating machines who were programmed to live 'virtuous' lives. Human life is valuable to the extent that it is self-determining. God has given his creatures the power to choose between good and evil and, in so doing, has taken the risk that many of them will in fact choose evil. This is the cost of free will. It is, therefore, human actions, not God's, which are responsible for the suffering in the world. On the other hand, the problem of human evil is more serious than that of natural disasters because, even if God is not directly responsible for suffering, he has created a situation where moral depravity can arise. This cannot be inadvertent: we cannot suppose that God has allowed evil to arise in the world through an *oversight*. For such a supposition would not only be inconsistent with God's omniscience, it would also leave unanswered the problem of why God continues to permit evil. It seems, then, that evil is part of God's design. This is an uncomfortable conclusion, but some theists have grasped the nettle. The line they take is that suffering is a necessary condition of our moral development as free agents. We cannot learn to behave with compassion unless we are given the power to make others suffer, and feel the effects of others' exercise of that power.

It is not so much the integration of evil into the divine design, important though that is, which is the concern of this chapter, but rather the relevance of human freedom to the problem of evil. For unless evil can appropriately be attributed to the exercise of our freedom, any attempt along these lines to justify evil must fail.

## DETERMINISM AND HUMAN NATURE

At first sight, the notion of an omnipotent God creating beings with free will seems paradoxical. If God is omnipotent, then there is nothing that he cannot control. Yet, if humans genuinely have free will – that is, their choices are not antecedently determined by God – then it seems there are some things, namely human actions, which God cannot control. But the appearance of paradox is specious. It is not that God *cannot* control human actions but that, in giving humans free will, he chooses not to control them. It is within his powers to intervene at any point and prevent a given action, or its consequences, from occurring, but he simply refrains from exercising those powers. Choosing not to exercise one's powers does not imply that one never really had them in the first place, so our free will is no threat to God's omnipotence.

There is, however, something odd about God's introducing a certain amount of risk into the realisation of his plan. Given that his aim is for humans to develop a sense of the difference between good and evil, and always to choose the good, rather than the evil course, would it not have been rational for him to determine that this would inevitably be the outcome? But in choosing not to predetermine our actions in this way, God leaves it open to chance whether his design will be realised or not. Sometimes we choose the good course, but many times we choose the evil course, and so God's plan is endlessly frustrated. Would a rational creator leave so much to chance? Well, he need not leave *everything* to chance. Even though he may not predetermine every single action, he may weigh the chances in his favour by determining the natures of human beings. And he determines their natures in such a way that they are more likely to choose the good over the evil. Or does he? It is a matter of opinion whether human nature really is like this. Anthony Storr's grim verdict in *Human Aggression* is now depressingly familiar:

> That man is an aggressive creature will hardly be disputed. With the exception of certain rodents, no other vertebrate habitually destroys

members of its own species. No other animal takes positive pleasure in the exercise of cruelty upon another of his own kind. We generally describe the most repulsive examples of man's cruelty as brutal or bestial, implying by these adjectives that such behaviour is characteristic of less highly developed animals than ourselves. In truth, however, the extremes of 'brutal' behaviour are confined to man; and there is no parallel in nature to our savage treatment of each other. The sombre fact is that we are the cruellest and most ruthless species that has ever walked the earth; and that, although we may recoil in horror when we read in newspaper or history book of the atrocities committed by man upon man, we know in our hearts that each one of us harbours within himself those same savage impulses which lead to murder, to torture and to war.

(Storr 1970, p. 9)

If this is an accurate portrait of human nature, then God was not simply taking a risk in creating humans as the executors of the divine plan; he was creating something that was almost bound to frustrate that plan. Is this not an appalling piece of negligence? But even if we are more optimistic than Storr, and concede that, while capable of greater cruelty than any other species, man is also capable of greater good (or is perhaps the only species which is capable of good action), there is still the problem of why God does not determine our natures so that we are *bound* to choose the good, even though tempted by the bad. The reply may be that this would be simply to create morally insignificant automata, with no free will, but this response is by no means obviously the right one. The debate now leads us to the long-standing metaphysical issue of the relationship between free will and determinism, so let us survey this issue before returning to the question of God's determination of human nature.

Let us imagine a snap-shot description of the universe taken at the present moment. It is an unusual snap-shot, in that it includes *everything* that is presently the case: not just what you happen to be wearing, but the weather in various regions of the world, the number and species of living things, the composition of the earth, the positions of the planets, the relative distance of galaxies, etc. Now let us suppose that every aspect of that description, down to the smallest detail, is fixed by what state the universe was in just *before* the snap-shot was taken. That is a picture of a deterministic universe. Stated a little more formally, the universe is deterministic if and only if, given the state of the universe at a particular moment and the laws of nature, there is only one possible history of the universe. That is, the laws of nature, together with what is the case at a

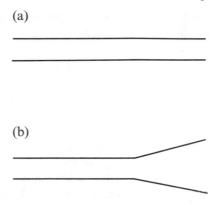

(a)

(b)

*Figure 7.1* Deterministic and indeterministic universes

particular moment, determine what will happen afterwards. We can represent the difference between deterministic and indeterministic universes pictorially.

Diagram (a) in Figure 7.1 represents two parallel universes with histories that exactly match each other: everything that happens in one at a particular time also happens in the other at a particular time. Diagram (b) represents universes whose histories are identical up to a certain point, but which diverge after that point. If two universes are deterministic, then (b) is an impossibility for them. If they have identical laws, and their histories match up to a certain point, they cannot diverge after that point: they must correspond to diagram (a). On the other hand, if they are *in*deterministic, (b) is a possibility: they could match perfectly up to a certain point, but then diverge thereafter.

How does the question of whether or not the universe is deterministic affect the issue of human freedom? There are two quite different conceptions of freedom, one of which is compatible with determinism, the other not. On one conception, an action of ours is free if and only if we could have done otherwise in the very same circumstances, and our choice to perform that action is free if and only if we could have chosen to do otherwise in those circumstances. If 'circumstances' here include the laws of nature and the state of the universe immediately prior to the choice, then this conception of freedom is not compatible with determinism, for those circumstances determine *everything* that happens afterwards, including the choice to perform that particular act and the subsequent action. So we could not have chosen or acted otherwise in those circumstances, though we might have chosen or acted otherwise if the circumstances had been different. On the second conception of freedom, an act is free simply if it is caused in the right kind of way, that is, by desires and intentions that are both ours and which predominantly reflect our nature. This is a 'negative' conception of freedom, in that it defines freedom as lack of constraint. If we move to a house in the country because the idea appeals to us, then that is a free action. If, while sitting on a chair with our legs crossed, we lift one leg rapidly because someone has tapped our knee with a hammer, that is not a free action. However, this negative view of freedom presents a continuum running from totally free to not at all free, rather than a clear, black and white distinction. If we hand over a large amount of cash because someone has threatened us with a revolver, is this action free or not? It is substantially less free than the move to the country, but, unlike the knee-jerk, it is an act over which we have intentional control. Vague though this conception of freedom is, it does correspond to our intuitive distinction between free and non-free actions, and it is also compatible with determinism. Even though my decision to live in the country may be wholly determined by the laws of nature and the state of the universe just prior to the decision, it is caused in the right kind of way: by my desires, beliefs and temperament.

To introduce some useful terminology, a *compatibilist* is one who believes determinism to be reconcilable with human freedom, and an *incompatibilist* is one who believes determinism to be irreconcilable with human freedom. The compatibilist will naturally adopt the second, 'negative' view of human freedom, whereas the incompatibilist will naturally adopt the first view. Neither the compatibilist nor the incompatibilist need take a stand on whether the universe is actually deterministic or not, but whereas the question need not worry the compatibilist, it will concern the incompatibilist. Most incompatibilists, wishing to hold on to the well-entrenched belief in human freedom (and perhaps also the freedom of higher animals), will suppose the universe to be indeterministic. The position which combines incompatibilism with belief in human freedom is known as *libertarianism*. (It is worth adding that nothing in science forces us to be determinists. Indeed, it has been suggested that physics in the twentieth century has presented us with a picture of the world as indeterministic.)

The libertarian needs to explain the difference between human actions and natural processes. Simply pointing to the fact (if it is a fact) that the universe is indeterministic will not do that. It may be true that, in the very circumstances in which we act, we could have acted differently. But then it is also true that, in the very circumstances in which my car engine failed to start this morning, it could have succeeded in starting: those circumstances did not necessitate its not starting, though they may have made it probable that it would not start. It is hard to see why the difference between a universe in which prior circumstances completely determine an event, and one in which they only make the event more probable, makes a moral difference, the difference between human freedom and human bondage. To see how the libertarian can distinguish free action from natural processes, we need to look more closely at the phrase 'could have done otherwise in the very same circumstances'. This must mean more than the unremarkable fact that it is logically possible for us to have acted in ways other than those in which we did act. It must mean that there is absolutely nothing constraining our choice among physically possible actions. Hence, agents are not simply one part of an enormous causal chain, but are the *origins* of causal chains. This, for the libertarian, is what distinguishes human action from the behaviour of other kinds of behaviour. Inanimate objects may not be determined to behave as they do, but they are *caused* to behave as they do by antecedent events. Not so human agents. Unless the incompatibilist is prepared to take this radical step of holding agents to be causally unconstrained, it is deeply obscure what makes human actions free and, say, the moves of your chess-playing computer not free. (Some incompatiblists, we should add, accept that human actions are not free, though this is not a popular position.)

## HUMAN FREEDOM FROM THE DIVINE PERSPECTIVE

Now let us return to the problem of suffering. If we are responsible for the suffering in the world, then we must be free agents, for otherwise it makes no sense to attribute responsibility to us. The theist now faces these questions: does God completely determine our actions? If he does not, are we free agents, or simply machines programmed to behave in a certain way? If he does indeed determine our actions, why does he determine that we act in such a way as to cause (apparently) needless suffering?

Let us try to look at the issue from God's point of view. Suppose he had made human nature such that we never chose to perform actions which would lead to needless suffering. Would there be any interest for God in such a project? Would it be any source of satisfaction to him to see us, time and time again, choose the steep and narrow path of right-eousness, rather than the broad path to perdition? Arguably not, for this is precisely how he would have programmed us. Our lives would develop utterly predictably, every action following from some initial state fixed by God. What, precisely, would be the point of creating such a universe? It would hardly realise any good, for it would be nothing more than an expression of God's own goodness. It seems that, for the universe to introduce any novelty, in the form of genuinely moral acts and decisions that are not simply the outcome of God's preprogramming, we must be free, in the more radical sense that we are able to choose to do otherwise even in the very same circumstances as the ones in which we made our choice. Thus, God is taking a risk, but it is a risk with a point: if we do choose the good, then that is really to our credit, and the existence of such choices is, it seems, a genuine advance on a universe without human creatures. It also looks as though we have an answer to Storr's bleak vision of humanity. The very fact that, morally, we are deeply flawed makes our virtuous actions all the more significant. The more base our natures, the more difficult the struggle to choose the good, and the greater the triumph when we do so choose.

This is, perhaps, the most convincing defence the theist can give in the face of man's inhumanity to man, but it is not one that is likely to appeal to the compatibilist. The compatibilist holds that our actions can be both free *and* determined. But our attempt to look at things from the divine perspective suggested that God is an incompatibilist: from God's point of view, there is no moral significance in creating human agents whose choices will simply follow his design to the letter. One might say that, for God, the significant kind of freedom is the first, whereby the agent can choose otherwise in the circumstances, whereas for the compatibilist, the significant kind is the second, whereby the act is caused in the right kind of way.

To see what difficulties compatibilism poses for theism, consider the possibility that God is a compatibilist (which is one way of saying that God exists and compatibilism is true). It would then be wrong to say that, if God wholly determined our actions, we would be, to him, morally insignificant automata. Then the theist would have to admit that it would be better if God determined our natures so that we always chose the good. Manifestly, it is not in our nature always to choose the good, so either God has deliberately chosen the worse course, or there is no being who has limitless powers to determine our nature. Neither of these conclusions is acceptable to the theist, so God, if he exists, cannot be a compatibilist. In other words, theism must embrace incompatibilism.

To reinforce the above remarks: compatibilism threatens any theistic justification of suffering. It will not do to say that suffering is necessary for the development of our moral personalities, and that is why God permits it. For if compatibilism is true, then God could have determined our moral personalities without making us suffer, and without infringing our freedom.

A number of different ideas have been in play here, and we have been oscillating from one position to another, so let us try to draw the threads of the discussion together so as to see more clearly the various positions open to the theist on the question of free will and God's responsibility for our actions. We can put two questions to the theist:

1 Is determinism (as we defined it above) compatible with our conception of human freedom or not?

2 If God completely determined human actions, would this make us mere automata in God's eyes, devoid of moral significance?

On the face of it, there are four possible responses. Each of them, it turns out, poses problems for the theist.

*First response:* Determinism is compatible with our conception of human freedom, but we would, in God's eyes, be mere automata if he completely determined our actions. What matters for us, then, is that our acts be caused in the right kind of way, namely by desires and intentions springing from our own nature. It does not matter what determines that nature.

This response implies that there is a difference between our conception of human freedom and God's, for, on this view, if God actually determined our actions, then we would, for God, be living under the quite illusory impression that we were free. But what is true from God's point of view must, for the theist, be the objective truth of the matter. Our conception of human freedom must be in line with God's.

The first response, then, must be rejected by the theist.

*Second response:* Determinism is *not* compatible with our conception of human freedom, but God would *not* regard us as automata if he completely determined our actions. The most efficient means of realising his purposes, therefore, would be for God to determine our actions completely.

Again, this response involves a conflict between the human and divine points of view, something the theist cannot allow. On this view, God's interests are best served by his completely determining our actions, and hence reducing us to what, in our view, would be morally insignificant automata. There is a further problem: if his interests are best served by completely determining our actions, then either he does in fact determine them, in which case he is directly responsible for the suffering in the world, or he does not, in which case he takes the irrational step of not doing what best serves his interests.

So the second response, too, must be rejected by the theist.

*Third response:* Determinism is compatible with our conception of human freedom, and God would *not* regard us as automata if he completely determined our actions. Again, the most efficient means of realising his purposes would be for God to determine our actions completely.

Here there is no conflict between the human and divine perspectives, and we can be held responsible for the suffering in the world, but some of the problems raised by the second response recur here. Either God does take the course which best realises his interests, in which case he is responsible for suffering (though only indirectly, by determining the actions of people who are directly responsible for it) and we have to conclude that the degree of suffering in the world is part of God's inscrutable design, or he does not take the course which best realises his interests, in which case he is irrational.

This response is coherent, but it does not succeed in distancing God from responsibility for suffering. He could have prevented evil without threatening our freedom. This third response must therefore be rejected by the theist.

*Fourth response:* Determinism is *not* compatible with our conception of human freedom, and we would, in God's eyes, be mere automata if he completely determined our actions. Presumably, then, he does not completely determine our actions because he desires us to be free, and we are therefore responsible for our actions. (I am assuming here that there is no room in theism for the view that we are not free. This assumption is surely justified for those versions of theism which make moral demands on us.)

Of all the four options, this seems to be the most promising line for the theist to take, as it fuses the human and divine perspectives – both of them incompatibilist, indeed libertarian, on this view – and it also distances God further from the amount of suffering in the world. Even if he intended some suffering (so that we would learn kindness and respect for others), he need not have intended *quite so much* suffering as in fact there is. There are still problems, however. We argued above that the libertarian needs to explain what distinguishes human actions from the behaviour of inanimate things, so that only the former are genuinely free. And we suggested that the only explanation the incompatibilist could give was that human agents, unlike inanimate objects, were not caused to act as they do. Now, if we take this line, we must hold that God is not even a remote cause of our actions. Our actions, literally, have nothing to do with God. Can the theist accept this? It certainly distances God yet further from suffering, because on this line God is not even an indirect cause of suffering. But if he is not causally responsible for the bad effects of our actions, he is not responsible for the good effects either. We would do nothing through his power. It would make no sense to call on God for strength to do right. Yet the idea of doing things through the grace of God is fundamental to theism.

There is a further problem. We can make sense of the idea of God creating human agents who are free in the negative sense, i.e. whose actions depend on their desires, etc. But can we make sense of God creating agents who are the causal originators of their actions? How is it possible for him to *make it the case* that human actions are caused by nothing but the agents which perform those actions? The fact that we have no idea how to answer these questions shows that libertarianism completely obscures God's role in the emergence of free agents in the world.

So, although the fourth response seems to be the best one for the theist to make, it is beset by difficulties, in that it makes entirely obscure the relation between God and human agency.

## CAN THE THEIST REFUSE TO ANSWER THE PROBLEM OF EVIL?

We have asked the question, 'Can suffering be justified on the theist picture?' I now want to ask, '*Should* it be justified?' Some theists believe that attempted justifications of suffering are, in a sense, complacent: they trivialise, or at best underplay, the degree of suffering in the world. The horrors of religious persecution under the Spanish Inquisition or in the reign of Mary I, the genocide of Hitler's regime, Stalin's treatment of the kulaks – these are simply too horrible to be explained away as the necessary, though regrettable, side-effects of the attainment of some greater good. Such theists take the view that it is a mistake to attempt to justify such suffering. We should, rather, trust to God that there is a reason for it which we simply cannot grasp. If belief in God is a matter of simple faith, not rational argument, then so too is the belief that God intends the best for us. The fact that we are beset by paradoxes when we try to reason about God is only evidence of our limited capacities, not of the fundamentally flawed nature of theism.

Before we ask whether this position is coherent, we should briefly explore a middle position between offering a full justification of suffering and avoiding the problem of evil altogether. We can distinguish between merely *explaining* suffering and *justifying* it. The theist can attempt to explain suffering by attributing it to the effects of free human action. This does not, however, justify it. To justify suffering, the theist needs to fit it into a view of God's purposes. The distinction, however, leaves open the possibility that explanation outruns justification. The theist who appeals to free will need not justify the worst excesses of human cruelty, in terms of the place it has in God's scheme of things, in order to explain why, in a world created by a loving God, there is such cruelty. The position the theist adopts will be that God is not responsible for these excesses, but any attempt by God to prevent them would be an infringement of human freedom. The discussion of the previous section, however, suggested that this middle position is not tenable. If we are compatibilists, then we will believe that our freedom is *not* infringed by God's determination of our action, so if God does not prevent suffering there must be some justification for it. If, on the other hand, we are incompatibilists, then the moral agent is completely independent of God – a view which is not at all congenial to theism. The theist, therefore, must believe that there is a justification of suffering, even if we have no access to that justification.

We should concede at the outset that the believer is not required to be a philosopher. It is no criticism of someone's faith that they cannot produce a watertight intellectual defence of their belief. Even in the absence of such rational support, their faith may be of the purest and most sincere kind. As we noted in the Introduction, it is an important issue, and one to which we shall return, whether rational justification is at all appropriate in a religious context. But, at the moment, we are engaged with a specific kind of believer, the putatively rational theist, whose faith is in part an attempt to answer intellectual problems of the 'why does anything exist?' kind, and also in part an attempt to account for objective moral values. Such a theist will understand the challenge of the problem of evil, and a refusal to answer the problem is not to be construed as the expression of a simple faith which does not look for rational justification, but a rational defence of what is taken to be a rational belief. If we can locate any inconsistency, or tension, within this defence, then we will have shown that this particular kind of theist is irrational.

There does, at least at first sight, appear to be an inconsistency in this approach to (or rather, retreat from) the problem of evil. On the one hand it is maintained that any attempted justification belittles suffering. This would seem to imply that, since suffering must be taken seriously, it has no justification. But, on the other hand, it is also maintained that suffering is not gratuitous: if we understood God's purposes, we would understand why there is – has to be – so much suffering in the world. Now this seems to imply that suffering *does* have a justification. So suffering both is, and is not, justified.

To get rid of the inconsistency, the theist's position may be further clarified as follows: the attempt to make suffering intelligible to limited, human intelligence inevitably belittles suffering. Nevertheless, were we to look at the matter from God's perspective (which we cannot do, even in principle), we would see that suffering *was* justified. We know this, because a loving God would not, without good reason, permit atrocious and gratuitous suffering.

This certainly removes the inconsistency, but at a high cost. As with certain approaches to human freedom, discussed in the previous section, a discrepancy has been introduced between the human perspective on things, and the divine perspective. Surely the whole point of the theistic outlook is the attempt to see things from God's point of view, and to free ourselves from the illusory perspective we are forced to adopt while immersed in the ephemera of human affairs. If it is impossible to adopt the divine perspective, then theism has nothing to tell us about the world and our place in it. But perhaps the most serious objection to this approach to the problem of evil is that it involves an admission that theism is irrational. Since this is a serious charge, I need to say something about what is involved in irrational belief.

The word 'rational' can be used in two quite different senses, an *external* sense and an *internal* sense. We sometimes say that belief in, say, astrology, is irrational. What we mean by this is that astrology conflicts with a 'scientific' picture of human personality. Now, if someone ignorant, or sceptical, of this scientific account persists in accepting astrological explanations, then the description of them as 'irrational' would be using the word in the external sense, meaning that their belief conflicts with some public, external, standard of acceptable thought. We might suggest that the alchemists were irrational, without wanting to imply that their standards of rational thought were the same as ours and that, by their own lights, they failed to match up to those standards. When someone is described as irrational in the internal sense, however, what is meant is that something has gone wrong in the way in which they have processed some information. For example, imagine someone learning of some personal catastrophe. Because the contemplation of the event is so awful, he persuades himself, perhaps unconsciously, that the event did not really happen, and so is guilty of self-deception. No-one thinks that self-deception is the way to acquire true beliefs, but some people nevertheless manage to deceive themselves. Such people fail to live up to their own standards of rationality: they are irrational by their own lights. If it turned out that the alchemists held beliefs which should not have survived their own standards of rationality, then we would be justified in describing them as irrational in the internal sense. A charge of internal irrationality is more serious than a charge of external rationality, because there is less excuse, if we can put it that way, for failing to apply one's own standards than for failing to apply someone else's.

Theists are often accused of irrationality by atheists. Now, if the accusation is that theists are irrational in the external sense, then theists have a comeback: they may question the standards of rationality adopted by the atheist, or the application of those standards to theistic belief. Much more serious is the accusation of *internal* irrationality, because this would be a problem intrinsic to theism. What I want to suggest is that theists who refuse to answer the problem of evil are guilty of internal irrationality, at least if they hold the following beliefs:

1   Belief in a loving creator is intellectually defensible.

2   We cannot solve the problem of evil; that is, we cannot explain how the existence and nature of suffering can be consistent with the existence of a loving creator.

Now, if, from the human perspective, belief in a loving creator cannot be squared with the presence of suffering, then it is simply not rational to continue to hold on to that belief. It is simply irrelevant that we can imagine *another* perspective in which there is no inconsistency between suffering and a loving creator. After all, we can imagine another perspective in which alchemy, or astrology, does not conflict with standards of rational thought: astrologers (presumably) are not irrational from their own perspectives. But, unless we are relativists, that is a reason for us to reject those perspectives as mistaken. Similarly, if, from our perspective, there is no justification for suffering, then that is a reason to reject, as mistaken, any perspective (including God's) in which there is a justification for suffering. If it turned out that, from God's perspective, any amount of human suffering is perfectly acceptable, that would be a horrible discovery to make. We simply could not go on believing that God was genuinely benevolent, at least as we conceive of benevolence. So, if we believe that theism can only be entertained if it is rational, and we believe that we cannot produce a satisfactory justification of suffering in terms of God's purposes, then we must reject theism. If the theist admits to (2), then (1) must be given up.

We shall end the chapter by citing an instance of the tension between beliefs (1) and (2), as it arises in the context of the teleological argument. The theist who believes the doctrine to be intellectually defensible may advance the teleological argument, if not as a fool-proof argument against atheism, at least as a consideration which makes theism highly attractive. The argument might be put in terms of a challenge to the atheist: what explanation can you offer of the order in the world which is as simple and satisfying as an explanation in terms of a benevolent deity? The universe is indeed ordered, the atheist might reply, but it also contains evil, and if you are looking for the best explanation of the universe you must take into account the presence of evil no less than the presence of order. This makes it far harder to infer the existence of a benevolent deity. A refusal to answer the problem of evil, then, considerably weakens the force of the challenge posed by the teleological argument. This was noted, and expressed with characteristic vividness, by Hume in the *Dialogues Concerning Natural Religion*, through the mouth of his character Philo:

> I will allow that pain or misery in man is compatible with infinite power and goodness in the Deity... what are you advanced by all these concessions? A mere possible compatibility is not sufficient. You must prove these pure, unmixt, and uncontrollable attributes from the present mixed and confused phenomena, and from these alone. A hopeful undertaking! Were the phenomena ever so pure and unmixed, yet, being finite, they would be insufficient for that purpose. How much more, where they are also so jarring and discordant!
>
> (Hume 1779, Part X)

## SUMMARY

The problem discussed in this chapter was the problem of reconciling the existence of a benevolent deity with the presence of evil in the world. If God intends us to suffer, then it seems he cannot be benevolent. On the other hand, if he does not intend us to suffer, then he is ineffective. Two strategies in dealing with this problem were examined: (a) the theist can try to distance God from direct responsibility for suffering by treating it as a consequence of the acts of free human agents; alternatively, (b) the theist can simply refuse to answer the problem on the ground that, although it must in God's eyes be justified, any attempted justification which we could produce simply trivialises suffering.

At first sight, (a) seems a promising strategy because it is plausible to suppose both that God wishes to create objects for his benevolence, and that he wishes such creatures to be genuinely free and not just automata. However, to understand (a) we need to be provided with an account of human freedom and its relation to determinism, the view that every state of the universe is fixed by some antecedent state. Two positions on this issue were defined: *compatibilism*, which holds that freedom is reconcilable with determinism, and *incompatibilism*, which holds that freedom cannot be reconciled with determinism. Here, however, we faced a dilemma. If we adopt compatibilism, then we admit that God could have created free agents while still determining our every action. But the question would then arise why God did not so determine things that we would avoid those acts which lead to unnecessary suffering. If, on the other hand, we adopt incompatibilism, then God could only create free agents by creating agents whose actions are uncaused. Apart from the obscurity of this idea, which involves the paradox of God's *causing* it to be the case that some things are *un*caused, it is in tension with the theistic belief that we can only do certain things through God's help.

The trouble with strategy (b) is that it threatens to make theism irrational. On the one hand, it is admitted that we cannot solve the problem of suffering, and that we are therefore unable to reconcile the obvious fact of suffering with belief in a benevolent God, and yet, on the other hand, we are supposed to hold on to belief in a benevolent God on the grounds that there *is* a justification for suffering which nevertheless is inaccessible to us. The question is whether we can be justified in assuming that there is such a justification. But we can only be justified in making this assumption if we are justified in our belief that there does exist a benevolent deity. But this is precisely what the problem of suffering casts into doubt. If theism is supposed to be a rationally defensible belief, this position is simply unintelligible.

## FURTHER READING

There are numerous discussions of the problem of evil. For a guide to the problem and a selection of essays on the topic, see Marilyn McCord Adams and Richard Merrihew Adams (eds), *The Problem of Evil* , Oxford: Oxford University Press, 1990.

Hume's striking presentation of the problem can be found in Part X of his *Dialogues Concerning Natural Religion*, ed. J.C.A. Gaskin, Oxford: Oxford University Press, 1993.

Examples of the attempt to reconcile suffering with the benevolence of God in terms of human freedom can be found in Basil Mitchell's *The Justification of Religious Belief*, London: Macmillan, 1973, and Richard Swinburne's *The Existence of God*, Oxford: Clarendon Press, 1979. Swinburne's account is criticised in Richard Gale's *On the Nature and Existence of God*, New York: Cambridge University Press, 1991.

For a helpful introduction to the issue of freedom and determinism, see Gary Watson (ed.), *Free Will*, Oxford: Oxford University Press, 1982.

# Part III
# Religion without God

# 8 Is God a fiction?

> *Faustus:* I think hell's a fable.
> *Mephistophilis:* Ay, think so still, till experience change thy mind.
>
> Marlowe, *Doctor Faustus*

## REALISM, POSITIVISM AND INSTRUMENTALISM

A standard response to the problem of evil is to reject theism altogether. There is no God, runs this response, and we should therefore seek a non-religious meaning in life and construct a morality which makes no reference to God. There is, however, another response, one which has become increasingly influential among theologians during the last few decades. Consider the 'therefore' of the sentence before last. If God does not exist as a real entity, responsible for the existence of the universe, does it follow that we should give up talk of God, and seek to inoculate ourselves against any religious influence on our affairs? Some writers have rejected this inference, and suggested that there is room for a different interpretation of talk about God. One difficulty with this position is that it is often couched in rather vague terms, encouraging the view that it is simply atheism dressed up in a few religious frills, the last refuge for one-time believers who cannot admit that they have lost their faith. In order to present this, in my view important, religious position with some precision, I shall make use of a debate in the philosophy of science over the status of theoretical entities. It will help us in our discussion, since it has not only been quite carefully defined by the contestants, but it also suggests a theological parallel.

Let us begin with the question, 'Do neutrons exist?' Now physicists do, of course, talk in terms of 'neutrons', are able to define them in relation to other entities ('A neutron is a component of the atom which has the same mass as a proton but carries no electric charge') and define laws governing their behaviour in processes like nuclear fission. But the question whether neutrons really exist amounts to more than the question whether physicists use the term 'neutron' in their theories. It concerns the issue of how such theories are to be interpreted. We can define three quite different interpretations. The first is called *realism*. According to realism (or 'scientific realism', if we are anxious to avoid confusion of this philosophical position with an attitude towards life or a movement in the history of art), scientific theories are to be taken at face value: if they appear to refer to entities in the world called 'neutrons', then this is what they in fact do, or at least what they are intended to do. Talk of neutrons is comparable to talk about more obviously mundane objects such as cars. We can define realism a little more formally in these terms: scientific theories are true or false by virtue of the way the world is, and independently of the ways we have of knowing about, or observing, the world. This last part may seem rather puzzling, but I hope it will be less so when we come to look at alternatives to realism. Note that realists are not also (necessarily) incorrigible optimists: they need not think that every theory currently espoused by physicists is bound to be true. Many, perhaps most, of those theories may be false. What is important is that, according to realism, theories about neutrons are capable of being true, and *if* they are true then there really are neutrons in the world.

In complete contrast to realism stands *instrumentalism*. Whereas the realist takes scientific theories at face value, as true or false descriptions of the world, the instrumentalist takes theories as non-descriptive, and consequently as neither true nor false. Theories, according to instrumentalism, are merely useful devices which we can manipulate in certain ways, in order to obtain, say, predictions about how things will behave. Theories are just fictions. In support of their position, instrumentalists may point to the widespread use of models in science. Consider, for example, the use of differently coloured balls to 'represent', as we would ordinarily say, atoms of different elements, and wires connecting the balls to 'represent' the bonds between atoms. Now, clearly, no-one thinks that this is what compounds really consist of: millions of little coloured balls joined together by wires. But by manipulating these models, we can make accurate predictions about how substances will interact with each other, and what the results of those interactions will be. A model, then, can be useful even if it does not correspond in any direct way with the world. The realist will have to concede this, but will argue that such models would not be useful if they did not correspond to some degree with the way the world is. That is, unless there really were such things as atoms and molecules, and models captured part of the truth about those entities, then we would not be able to use models as predictive devices. If our theories really were purely fictional, the realist insists, their extraordinary success would be quite miraculous. The instrumentalist will simply reject this argument. Usefulness, for him, does not imply correspondence to reality, and he can support this still further by pointing to the use of *incompatible* models in science. The standard example of this is provided by the wave and particle models of light. In some respects, light behaves like the waves on a surface of water, and so can be modelled by such waves. In other respects, it behaves like a stream of particles, and so can be modelled by discrete objects. Now it is simply not possible for both of these models to correspond, except in the most abstract way, with reality, so, argues the instrumentalist, we may as well give up the notion of correspondence. Light can be modelled both by waves and by particles, but this says nothing about what light is really like.

It is useful to distinguish this rather extreme instrumentalism, which holds that theories do not describe the world, and are neither true nor false, from a more moderate position which says, in effect: 'For all we know, our theory may be true, but we can use it without making any assumptions about its truth. Truth does not matter, only usefulness. And this is just as well, for we could never discover whether a theory is really true – we have no privileged perspective on reality which allows us to judge this – but we can certainly discover whether or not a theory is useful.' This more moderate position is sometimes described as *epistemological instrumentalism*.

The final position we shall look at is *positivism*. The positivist agrees with the realist's assertion that theories are either true or false (and so disagrees with the instrumentalist in this respect), but denies that theories are to be taken at face value. Consider the neutron again. Neutrons are supposed to be sub-atomic, and hence invisible, entities. The realist is quite happy to believe in the existence of those entities, even though their existence has to be inferred from what we can perceive, rather than (more or less) directly given to us in perception. The positivist, in contrast, will not grant that we can talk about things that we could not possibly observe. The real meaning of statements supposedly about invisible neutrons is given by the experimental outcomes: the meter-readings, the traces on a VDU screen, the clicks of a Geiger counter. We can talk, according to the positivist, only of what we can observe. So, when physicists are apparently talking about neutrons, what they are using is a kind of code, a shorthand, for information about what can be observed in the laboratory. On the other hand, when they are apparently talking about their cars, they really *are* talking about their cars. This, I hope, makes less cryptic the formal definition of realism given above. We defined the realist view as follows: scientific theories are true or false in virtue of the way the world is, *independently of the ways we have of knowing about, or observing, the world.* The positivist will accept the first part of this, but reject the part in italics. Positivism does not accept that our theories could be true independently of what we can observe, because what the theories are about is, precisely, what we can observe.

Positivism is not, currently, a popular position among philosophers of science. The main difficulty with it is that, when we try to spell out what, in detail, a given scientific statement means in terms of the observable, we find that there are simply too many candidates for the job. In fact, for every theoretical statement, there will be an infinite number of statements about what we would observe in certain circumstances. Take the statement, 'The pressure in the container is 25 atmospheres'. This may seem to be a straightforward observation, but in fact the term 'pressure' is a theoretical one, related as it is in this context to the more obviously theoretical idea of the number of molecules of gas per cubic metre of volume. And, quite clearly, we cannot observe pressure directly: it is something we have to measure. Now, for the positivist, what the statement 'The pressure in the container is 25 atmospheres' actually means, what it stands for, can be presented as a rather more complex statement about what can be directly observed, namely the reading on the pressure gauge. But here, now, is the problem: what kind of gauge are we talking about? Is pressure to be measured in terms of the level of fluid in a mercury barometer, or by the position of the needle in an aneroid barometer, or indirectly through knowledge of the original volume of gas in an uncompressed state and the temperature before and after compression, or by some other method? It would be quite arbitrary to settle on just one of these as providing the true meaning of the statement about pressure. Clearly, we must include them all. So 'The pressure in the container is 25 atmospheres' will be replaced, in the final analysis, by something like 'The mercury level is at $n$, or the needle points to $m$, or ..., etc.' But since there are an indefinite number of ways in which pressure can be measured, the new sentence will be indefinitely long. But is it plausible to suggest that we can only grasp the meaning of a finite, theoretical sentence by grasping the meaning of an infinite, non-theoretical sentence?

That concludes our brief tour of the chief positions in this particular debate in the philosophy of science. We need not enter into the detail of the arguments for each, since we have introduced them only in order to draw a parallel with the debate about the existence of God. Even so, the problems facing scientific positivism, sketched above, are worth bearing in mind when we turn to its theological counterpart.

# RADICAL THEOLOGY

Corresponding to realism in science is realism in theology. Thus, *theological realism* is the view that statements apparently about God should be taken at face value, that is, as intended to be used to refer to a transcendent being. Such statements are descriptive and so are true or false. Now, whereas 'scientific realism' is assumed to be agnostic about the truth of scientific theories, the term 'theological realism' is often used to define the position of the traditional theist: not only are theistic statements capable of being true, they actually *are* true. I shall, however, reserve the term for the more cautious theory. In this sense the traditional atheist can be called a theological realist. He thinks that, although theistic statements are intended as descriptive and hence are capable of being true, they are actually false. Much of the discussion of the previous chapters has proceeded on the assumption of theological realism. That is, it has taken theism as a hypothesis about what the world really contains. As such, it has been found to be defective. We can, in response to this, stay within theological realism and adopt atheism in the traditional sense. Or we can, instead, reject theological realism altogether, and accept the old theistic language, but under a new interpretation. This second response is the project of radical theology.

'Radical theology' is not the name of a single doctrine, but of an approach to theological language and religious practice. Or rather, it is the name of a set of approaches, for many writers, using quite different methods and idioms, have been described as 'radical'. To anchor the discussion, therefore, I am going to choose one contemporary radical theologian who has become particularly prominent in recent years: Don Cupitt. His writings provide a clear and accessible account of the radical theologian's rejection of theological realism. Even so, there is a crucial ambiguity in his statement of the non-realist position, and we can draw this out by reflecting on the distinction between scientific instrumentalism and scientific positivism.

Instrumentalism, recall, takes theories to be fictions, adopted because they are useful, not because they are true descriptions of the world. Positivism takes them to be descriptions, not of what they appear to refer to, but of what is immediately available to us in experience. Stated in these abstract terms, they can be applied to statements apparently about God. Thus we can define *theological instrumentalism* as the view that discourse about God is purely fictional. Not only hell, but heaven as well, are fables. The point of reflecting on stories about God is not, obviously, that we are thereby enabled to predict the behaviour of the cosmos, but rather that our lives will be transformed. By having an image of the goodness of God before us, we will be encouraged to lead a less selfish, and therefore more fulfilling, life. The *idea* of God, rather than God himself, is thus an instrument through which good can be realised. *Theological positivism* shares with instrumentalism the view that theistic discourse does not refer to a transcendent deity, but differs in that it does not take such discourse to be fictional. Discourse apparently about God is true, on the positivist view, but what it describes, in symbolic language, are truths about our moral and spiritual (some would say our psychological) lives. Theistic language is really moral language in coded form.

Now instrumentalism and positivism are quite different, and indeed incompatible, philosophical positions. Nevertheless, it is possible to find both positions apparently represented in radical theology – indeed, in the writings of a single theologian. To illustrate this, I offer the following quotations from Cupitt's very influential book, *Taking Leave of God* (1980):

1   God is a unifying symbol that eloquently personifies and repre-
    sents to us everything that spirituality requires of us.

    (p. 9)

2   [The spiritual life is] orientated towards a focus imaginarius.

    (p. 10)

3   The Christian doctrine of God just is Christian spirituality in
    coded form.

    (p. 14)

4   We use the word 'God' as a comprehensive symbol that incorpo-
    rates the way that the religious demand presents itself to us.

    (p. 96)

5   The only religiously adequate God cannot exist.

    (p. 113)

6   ... the suffering God ... is merely the tears and the fellow-feeling
    of humanity.

    (p. 113)

7   God is a myth we have to have.

    (p. 166)

Compare the first, third, fourth and sixth quotations above with the second, fifth and seventh. The first groups appear to point quite definitely to positivism. Note the words 'symbol' and 'coded form'. Note also that Christian ideas are identified with moral and spiritual ones: the doctrine of God *just is* Christian spirituality; the suffering God *is* the tears of humanity. The quotations in the second group, however, appear to point just as definitely to instrumentalism: God is a 'focus imaginarius', a 'myth', he cannot (really) exist.

There is at least a tension here, and it should be resolved. Should we try to reduce theistic statements to non-theistic ones and reveal their true meaning? Or should we leave them as they are, but treat them as make-believe? The first of these is the less attractive option. First, it leaves the radical theologian open to the charge that his position is just a disguised form of atheism. Since moral language can be autonomous, i.e. it does not need to be presented as part of a religious package and make essential reference to God, why can we not just restrict ourselves to that language and give up the rather misleading 'coded' version which talks of deity, judgement, salvation and damnation? Second, we should remember the trouble with scientific positivism. When we try to specify just which statements about measurement we should replace the theoretical statements with, we find there are just too many to include. Is it not likely that theological positivism will find itself in similar difficulties? That is, there may be an infinite number of moral meanings to read into any piece of doctrine. And when we are dealing, not with doctrine, but with some more specific statement about God's actions, as related in some religious text, we may be entirely at a loss to locate any hidden moral meanings.

In theology, as in science, instrumentalism is far more plausible than positivism. It also makes the interpretation of radical theology easier, for it is possible to give an instrumentalist reading of even the positivistically flavoured quotations from Cupitt. Take the idea of God as a symbol of the religious demand. We might think of this along the lines of symbols in fiction. When we say that Scrooge's clerk, Bob Cratchit, in Dickens's *A Christmas Carol*, is a symbol of cheerfulness in adversity, we might be pointing to an ideal that Dickens himself had, and represented by various characters. We do not mean to imply that every statement apparently about Bob Cratchit is really a statement about how one ought to behave under certain circumstances. Similarly, characters in religious fictions may serve to represent certain religious ideals.

Let instrumentalism, then, be our model for understanding radical theology. We now come up against a problem. If talk about God is purely fictional, how is it that it can exert an influence on our lives? If it is only fictionally true that God requires us to lead a certain life, why should we respond to that requirement? One aspect of the way in which religious discourse can help to shape our lives seems relatively unproblematic. We are familiar with parables: stories about concrete situations which are supposed to illustrate more abstract morals. If we were simply told the moral, in abstract terms, then, while perhaps agreeing with it, or making a note to live in accordance with it, we would not perhaps be as strongly influenced by it as we would by a story which conveyed the same message in dramatic terms, and in which various properties such as pride, jealousy, or foolhardiness are represented by a character. The concrete has far greater impact than the merely abstract. Now the radical theologian might be saying this: *all* religious discourse is a parable. In Christianity, for example, God is a concrete figure in a story, representing, among other things, parental virtues. The crucifixion, burial of Christ, and the subsequent discovery of the empty tomb are concrete images representing the transformation of our spiritual life through suffering.

But this view of religious discourse as a series of parables cannot be a complete account of religion because it ignores the more active aspects of religious life. Religion is not merely a matter of listening passively to stories with a point to them; it involves us in such activities as worship, prayer, the taking of vows, confession and contemplation. Religion engages not merely our intellect but our emotions. The radical theologian, therefore, needs to explain precisely what we are doing when we are engaged in religious activity which appears to be directed towards a deity. If the correct understanding of religious doctrine is an instrumentalist one, how is it that we can become emotionally involved in religious worship? It might be said that there is no difficulty here. After all, we are familiar with the experience of being moved by fiction. We can sympathise with, pity or feel revulsion at fictional goings-on, even while recognising that they are fictional. And the emotions generated by fiction can be channelled so as to affect the interactions we have with other people. In sympathising with a character facing some great dilemma, we may come to understand better how to deal with the dilemmas of ordinary life. Can religion not exploit this familiar phenomenon? To discover whether it can, we need to understand just how it is possible that fiction can exert an effect on our emotions and, through our emotions, our actions. And when we have come to understand that, we must ask whether the power of religious discourse need really be nothing more than an instance of the power of fiction, or whether some important dissimilarities remain.

## FICTION AND THE EMOTIONS

'It's only a story' is a familiar refrain, used to soothe a child (or even an adult) upset by some tale of misfortune. The implication is that, once we realise that something has not really happened, we no longer have a reason to fear, or feel sad about it. This is certainly true in cases where we have simply been misled. Believing falsely that someone has walked off with my umbrella after a party on a rainy night, I am relieved to find it hidden under a pile of coats. But this hardly explains why we become emotionally involved with something we recognise to be fiction. If someone is in tears by the end of a novel which ends sadly, this is not, typically, because they falsely believe the novel to be stating the truth. Here, the blithe remark 'It's only a story' may have no effect on the reader's feelings. We may be sufficiently concerned for the safety of some innocent character as to feel real anxiety when we read of her walk through a lonely forest in thick fog, and relieved when no harm in fact befalls her. Or, just as some hideous creature lunges at her from out of the darkness, we may feel similar relief when, in the novel, she wakes up and we realise that it has all been a dream.

Is there not something highly paradoxical, however, in fearing something that we know to be false? The character never was in any danger because, quite simply, she does not exist. Similarly, we are in absolutely no danger from the man who dresses up as his mother and murders the woman in the shower in Hitchcock's film *Psycho*. Yet we may, for a short while after seeing the film, be somewhat reluctant to take a shower. Why is this? Two ways of dispelling the paradox suggest themselves. One is that, for a fleeting moment, we forget that we are reading, hearing or watching, a fiction, and believe that we really are being presented with the truth. It is this belief which causes our emotion. But this suggestion is surely wrong. Typically, when we feel fear as a result of some belief that, say, we are in danger, we will be inclined to do something about it. Fearing that we really are in danger from the man in *Psycho*, we would take steps to find out where he is operating, or whether he has been caught. We would take care to keep the doors locked, even during the day, and especially when taking a shower. But fiction does not incline us to action in this direct way. We watch the film without running out of the cinema and ringing the police, or buying a paper to find out the latest. We are not fooled, even for a moment. Further, if we only lose our hold on reality for a moment, and only instantaneously believe the fiction to be true, then, on this account, our emotional state should be correspondingly fleeting. But, typically, our emotions will not fluctuate in this way.

A second, more plausible, suggestion is that fiction generates emotions by bringing to our attention genuine, although quite general, truths. The novels of Dickens bring to our attention the appalling conditions in which the poor lived in Victorian England, and, to a lesser extent, the conditions of the poor today. A science fiction story may start us pondering on how little we know about the possibility of intelligent, and perhaps malevolent, life beyond the solar system. A novel about troubled family relationships may set us thinking about our own troubled family relationships, and thus evoke guilt, anger or sadness.

There is certainly an element of truth in this suggestion, but it cannot be the whole story. The emotions generated by a fiction can be quite acute, but are likely to be relatively short-lived. They may last only as long as the fiction is engaging our immediate consciousness. In contrast, the emotions we feel when contemplating the general issues that fiction may bring to our attention are, unless they concern us directly, likely to be somewhat less acute and last for a longer period of time. Another shortcoming of this account is that it suggests that the true object of our emotions is *not* the fictional character, but some state of affairs in the world which is suggested by the fictional situation. This does not do justice to our experience of fiction, for the immediate object of our emotion *is*, surely, the fictional character. We really are frightened *for* the character picking her way through the dark, menacing, mist-shrouded forest, and not, or not just, for anyone who might happen to be in this situation. We really are sorry *for* the couple in *Brief Encounter* who, out of loyalty to others, part for ever. It is the imaginary characters themselves, not the real situations they symbolise, who have such an immediate call on our feelings.

A third account has been put forward by Kendall Walton, a philosopher who has written extensively and influentially on the nature of our relation to fiction (Walton 1978a and b). He proposes that, when we become involved in a fictional story, we are engaging in a game of make-believe. Just as a child make-believes that a group of chairs set in a line is a bus, or that, in chasing after a friend, he is chasing after a desperate criminal, armed to the teeth with a pop-gun and a water-pistol, so we, in reading a novel, make-believe that it is reporting the truth. In doing so we, as it were, locate ourselves in the novel. We are there, witnessing the events. We may even assign ourselves a role, and imagine talking to the characters. It is our active participation in the fiction, suggests Walton, which explains why we become emotionally involved. A child engaged in a make-believe game of cops and robbers may become very excited, and run about shrieking with apparent fright. Indeed, the make-believe can increase the intensity of the experiences generated by what would otherwise be an ordinary game of hide-and-seek. The physiological responses may be the same as those of real fear. But, says Walton, there is a difference. A child who make-believes that a child-devouring creature is after it will not, unless something is wrong, feel genuine fear, for otherwise the child would not want to participate in the game. But the emotion is close enough to real fear for us to call it quasi-fear. Similarly, we will experience quasi-anxiety when watching a thriller on the television: if it were genuine anxiety we would probably switch it off. By analogy, we should describe the emotions evoked by *Brief Encounter* as quasi-pity and quasi-sadness. If so, however, it is apparent that these supposedly *ersatz* emotions are closer to their *echte* counterparts than is quasi-fear to real fear. After all, quasi-sadness can lead to real tears. But still, the emotion is not a wholly unpleasant one, and we are not left in a state of black gloom when the woman who has just said good-bye to her lover is left desolate in the waiting room. In short, then, Walton's solution of the paradox that we can be emotionally involved in something we know to be false is that we play a game of make-believe in which the fiction becomes reality, and part of the game is to feel something akin to real emotions, though they are not the genuine article.

Are there any further approaches we might take to deal with the paradox? We might just pause for a moment to reflect on how the three strategies above arise. There are essentially three components to the paradox. The first is the belief state we are in when engaging with fiction, namely the belief that the fiction is false. The second is the emotional state generated by the fiction: fear, pity, or whatever. The third is the object of the emotion, namely the fictional character. Now each of the three strategies above modifies a different component of the paradox. The first modifies the belief: we do not, in fact, believe that the fiction is false. The second account modifies the emotional object: the true object of our emotion is not the fictional character, but rather some person or situation in the real world. The third, Walton's account, modifies the emotional state: it is not real fear/anxiety/pity but only quasi-fear, etc. Since there are just these three components to the paradox, it would seem that the three strategies (or some combination of them) for dealing with it exhaust the possibilities.

There is, however, a fourth strategy, and that is not to modify *any* of the components but to insist that it is not paradoxical for us to become emotionally involved with a situation we know not to obtain. We might offer various explanations for this. One is that the emotional state is a more-or-less automatic response to the fictional presentation: we see an unhinged murderer lurking in the darkness on the cinema screen and immediately feel fear. This account depends on there being some dissociation between our emotions and our beliefs, to the extent that we cannot consciously control our emotions. This runs somewhat contrary to empirical research conducted in the early 1960s, which concluded that, although our physiological responses to a situation could be quite automatic, our emotional states are largely determined by how we interpret the situation, and what we identify as the cause of our physiological reaction.

Thus, armed with a number of suggestions as to how fiction can influence the emotions, we can turn to the question of how we should understand participation in religious activity.

## ATHEISM AND RELIGIOUS PRACTICE

In *A Path from Rome*, Anthony Kenny describes the doubts and conflicts which eventually led to his leaving the Catholic priesthood. He also tells us that, in spite of his agnosticism, he continued to attend church regularly, though never receiving Communion or reciting the Creed. He did this, not to pretend to a faith which he no longer had, but because of the important role that certain religious practices, including prayer, can continue to have even in the life of someone who has given up firm belief in theism. In an earlier book, *The God of the Philosophers*, he compares the agnostic at prayer to someone 'adrift in the ocean, trapped in a cave, or stranded on a mountainside, who cries for help though he may never be heard or fires a signal which may never be seen' (Kenny 1979, p. 129). Just as there is nothing unreasonable in this latter activity, the implication is, so there is nothing unreasonable in the former: the agnostic does not know whether there is anyone listening to his prayer, but there is a chance that there is, and that the prayer will be answered.

What, for Kenny, justifies prayer does not extend to saying the Creed. Kenny's position is clearly a realist one, which implies that when one says 'I believe in God, the father Almighty, maker of heaven and earth . . . ' one is stating what one intends to be the literal truth. An agnostic cannot utter these words without either hypocrisy or self-deception. This defence of a rather limited range of religious practices – just those which do not definitely commit one to any theistic doctrine – would not be accepted by the theological instrumentalist. If religion has a point, it is not, for the instrumentalist, because it *might*, for all we know, be true. It is neither true nor false. What is needed, for instrumentalism to be a viable theological position, is a defence of religious practice which allows an atheist, someone who believes that, realistically construed, theism is false, to engage in worship and prayer. I suggest that such a defence can be found in comparing the effects of religion to the beneficial effects of fiction. Of the four accounts of our emotional response to fiction that we considered in the previous section, the most plausible, I suggest, is Walton's. So let us apply Walton's account to religious practice.

To engage in religious practice, on this account, is to engage in a game of make-believe. We make-believe that there is a God, by reciting, in the context of the game, a statement of belief. We listen to what make-believedly are accounts of the activities of God and his people, and we pretend to worship and address prayers to that God. In Walton's terms, we locate ourselves in that fictional world, and in so doing we allow ourselves to become emotionally involved, to the extent that a religious service is capable of being an intense experience. The immediate object of our emotions is the fictional God, but there is a wider object, and that is the collection of real individuals in our lives. In the game of make-believe (for example, the Christian one), we are presented with a series of dramatic images: an all-powerful creator, who is able to judge our moral worth, to forgive us or to condemn, who appears on Earth in human form and who willingly allows himself to be put to death. What remains, when the game of make-believe is over, is an awareness of our responsibilities for ourselves and others, of the need to pursue spiritual goals, and so on.

How adequate is this account? A number of difficulties present themselves:

1 This justification of religious practice seems far less powerful than the one which is available to the realist, for whom prayer and worship really is God-directed, and for whom the emotions thus evoked are real, capable of having a direct effect on one's life. The instrument-alist, in contrast, has to make do with Walton's quasi-emotions: a make-believe imitation of the real thing. Is such a watered-down version of religious practice worth preserving?

2 In reading fiction as fiction, one is simply following the designs of the author, who is inviting one to participate in a game of make-believe. The authors of religious documents and rituals were not, surely, invariably issuing such an invitation (though some religious writing is explicitly fictional). To treat all religion as make-believe is arguably a perversion of its original purpose.

3 Any given fiction is a relatively fleeting thing: it is not possible to sustain a game of make-believe indefinitely. Yet religion is not merely something to dip into. To lead a religious life is to have certain images almost constantly in front of one, informing one's activities. How could the religious picture be sustained, if it were not taken to be a reflection of reality?

Let us take these points in order.

The instrumentalist can answer the first point by pointing out that the realist justification of religious practice is an option that has already been rejected, on the grounds that theological realism is untenable. If theological realism is itself a highly problematic position, it can hardly provide an adequate justification of any practice based on it. The instrumentalist justification of religious practice is superior, simply because it is not based on dubious metaphysical assumptions. But there is still the point about emotions. Against the instrumentalist is the consideration that someone who believes in the literal truth of what is said in a religious ritual will, surely, experience genuine emotions which, because they are genuine, are far more likely to have an impact on their life than the quasi-emotions generated in a game of religious make-believe. What can be said about this? The true (i.e. in this context, the realist) believer will be motivated not just by the emotions caused by religious ritual but also by his beliefs. Now, if the instrumentalist is right, some of those beliefs, namely those concerning the literal truth of religious doctrines, are false, and therefore give rise to a degenerate kind of spiritual life. The effect of a literal faith on one's life may actually be (in part) a negative one. For example, recall the argument of Chapter 6: if we perform an act because we believe God wills it, then we are not genuinely autonomous agents: we abdicate the responsibility of deciding for ourselves what is right.

The second point draws attention to historical issues. What were the intentions of those responsible for religious writings and observances? Were they concerned to report, in unambiguous terms, a generally agreed set of truths? Or were they attempting to convey, in allegorical terms, ideas whose content was quite nebulous? Did they devise rituals whose purpose was to provide an appropriate setting for the promulgation of true propositions and for direct communion with God? Or was the purpose rather to exploit the aesthetic and dramatic impact of a communal activity, perhaps accompanied by music, and perhaps also in a place of size and beauty? Was it a combination of these, not necessarily conflicting, purposes? When we consider that the authors concerned were not a small group of contemporaries, but a large group scattered over the centuries and from a variety of cultures, the difficulty of giving a single clear answer to these questions becomes obvious. But this much is true: it is inconceivable that religious writings and rituals are not, to some extent, works of the imagination. This is so even if we accept the realist approach to theism. If there is a creator of the universe, then our ways of conceiving him still require imaginative effort. Even the realist, in explaining the impact of religion, must exploit the effect exerted on us by fiction and make-believe.

Let us now turn to the third point, on the transience of fiction and the permanence of religion. The contrast is, in fact, an entirely specious one. It is true that engagement with fiction is occasional. We read a book, become involved in it, finish it, continue to reflect on it for a time, but then become immersed in other activities, perhaps returning to the book after a few years. But then religion, too, is an occasional thing. Formal religious observance may take place once a day, but it is more likely to be once a week, once a year, or even less frequently than that. Of course, religious reflection can take place outside of a formal setting, but even then, other activities and concerns intervene. Still, it might be urged, although it is occasional, religious involvement can be a life-long thing. But then we do not have to look far to find a fictional parallel. Televised soap operas may only last half an hour and are broadcast one, two or three times a week, but they go on apparently indefinitely. As viewers of these programmes, we may continue to engage with a single fiction for years on end. It may, in fact, come to occupy a considerable portion of our thoughts, and the moral status of the various fictional goings-on may become a topic of animated discussion week after week. And if we eventually tire of these fictions, it is only because they lack the richness and complexity of religion, not because they are merely fictional. The constancy of religion is a testament to its dramatic power, not to its veracity.

Finally, I want to consider the objection that theological instrument-alism does not, after all, avoid the pitfalls it was intended to avoid. The general idea here is that, if a certain proposition is incoherent, then treating it as fictional will not make it coherent. To be more specific, let us think again about two moral arguments for atheism introduced in Part II. One was the problem of evil: how could a loving God permit suffering when he is in a position to prevent it? The other was the problem of moral autonomy: if I act simply because I believe that God wills me to act, then I am not truly autonomous, and am not acting for moral reasons. Do these problems not arise even if we treat religion as a game of make-believe? Let us look at them in turn.

Even if it is only fictionally the case that God is perfectly loving and all-powerful, then it is still *fictionally* the case that he permits suffering which he could have prevented. There is thus an apparent tension within the fiction itself. However, since we not only participate in, but also to some extent create, the game of make-believe, we can choose what to include in it. We may well include the idea of suffering. Indeed, for most theistic outlooks, suffering plays an important role in spiritual develop-ment. But we do not need to include the idea that the world contains an appalling amount of apparently pointless suffering. We will, in fact, simply avoid introducing anything which would result in tensions within the fiction. The counterpart of this manoeuvre within the realist scheme of things would be to shut our eyes to the state of things, so that it does not disturb our faith. That manoeuvre, however, looks far less acceptable.

What of the issue of autonomy? If I imagine God's requiring me to act in a particular way, and act because of that imagined requirement, then I am no more acting for truly moral reasons than if I act because I think God really is requiring me to do so. Although the requirement is only fictional, I am acting, it seems, as if I were not an autonomous agent. But this objection, too, is misplaced. The make-believe game in which I pretend that God is requiring me to do certain things does not affect my actions directly. Rather, in engaging with the game, I am led to certain true (not fictional) beliefs about what I ought to do. It is these beliefs on which I act, and I do so as a fully autonomous agent. When I decide what to do, I no longer do it on the basis of some make-believe requirement, but on a requirement I come to recognise when I play the game of make-believe. In general, fiction may influence the way we act, but our reasons for so acting need not involve any fictional beliefs.

Our account of religion as fiction, then, need not generate the problems which beset realism.

In this chapter, we have presented theological instrumentalism simply as a defensible alternative to traditional atheism, which takes a realist approach to theistic statements and rejects them as false. In the next chapter, we shall examine an argument to the effect that instrumentalism is the only option.

## SUMMARY

Unable to resolve the difficulties which theism raises, we may choose to reject it altogether. There is, however, an alternative response, and that is to reconstrue theism along non-realist lines. We may continue to employ religious language, even if we do not take it to be a direct reflection of reality. This is the path taken by radical theology. In the first part of this chapter, we explored two models taken from the philosophy of science which define quite different non-realist approaches. One of these is positivism, which, in a religious context, holds that statements apparently about God are equivalent in meaning to statements about moral requirements. The other is instrumentalism, which regards theistic statements as fictional, and religious observance as a form of make-believe. It was suggested that instrumentalism was a more satisfactory route for the radical theologian to take than positivism.

The radical theologian, however, must explain how the moral impact of religion, and therefore the point of religious observance, is not undermined by the abandonment of realism. Why should we continue to talk in theistic terms if theism is not really true? One answer to this exploits the well-known emotional response to fiction. Although we understand that fiction is not a true description of reality, we can nevertheless become emotionally involved with it, and, through this involvement, our lives in the real world can be transformed. There is an apparent paradox here, that of fearing, pitying or loving things we know not to exist, but, once we have resolved the paradox, we can present a coherent account of the benefits of religion in a community of non-believers. The superficial disanalogies between fiction and religion do not threaten this defence of religion without belief.

## FURTHER READING

A useful discussion of realism, instrumentalism and positivism in the philosophy of science which highlights the problems faced by non-realist theories can be found in Chapter 2 of W.H. Newton-Smith's *The Rationality of Science*, London: Routledge & Kegan Paul, 1981. Another useful source is Bas van Fraassen, *The Scientific Image*, Oxford: Clarendon Press, 1980, Chapter 1.

There are a number of books by Don Cupitt which express different aspects of his radical theology, but perhaps the most direct and accessible is *Taking Leave of God*, London: SCM Press, 1980. A less austere introduction to radical theology is his *The Sea of Faith*, London: BBC Publications, 1984, which is enriched by compelling discussions of a number of historical figures who felt obliged to abandon, or at least to question, traditional theological thinking. Cupitt's rejection of virtually all forms of realism, based on his conception of language, is articulated in *The Last Philosophy*, London: SCM Press, 1995.

Other statements of non-realist approaches to religion can be found in the works of D.Z. Phillips. See especially *The Concept of Prayer*, London: Routledge & Kegan Paul, 1965, and *Religion Without Explanation*, Oxford: Basil Blackwell, 1976. An early philosophical statement of the non-realist approach can be found in Richard Braithwaite's 'An Empiricist's View of the Nature of Religious Belief', reprinted in Basil Mitchell (ed.), *The Philosophy of Religion*, Oxford: Oxford University Press, 1971, pp. 72–91. Interestingly, Phillips distances himself from Braithwaite's statement of the position.

Kendall Walton's article 'Fearing Fictions', in *Journal of Philosophy* 65 (1978), pp. 5–27, provides a lively account of our emotional response to fiction. The status of fictional 'worlds' is treated in more detail in his 'How Close are Fictional Worlds to the Real World?', *Journal of Aesthetics and Art Criticism* 37 (1978), pp. 11–23.

# 9    Is 'Does God exist?' a real question?

The Elimination of Metaphysics
                    Title of a chapter in A.J. Ayer, *Language, Truth and Logic*

## THE DEFLATIONIST ARGUMENT

*Ontological questions* are concerned with what exists, or rather, with what general kinds of thing exist. So, for example, 'Are there ghosts?' is an ontological question which both philosophers and non-philosophers might ask. The question is of interest to the philosopher because the existence of ghosts would imply the existence of disembodied beings, and this in turn might imply something interesting about our relationship to our own bodies. Most ontological questions posed by philosophers, however, would not occur to someone with no interest in philosophy. 'Are there physical objects?', for example, would seem a strange question to most people, but is of intense interest to philosophers, who might answer: 'No. Objects are nothing more than ideas.' And there are yet stranger ontological questions, such as 'Are there numbers?', and 'Would there be such a thing as redness if no red object existed?'

It is an important and difficult issue how we should understand ontological questions. Should we construe them as we would more ordinary questions of existence, such as 'Is there a bottle of wine in the cupboard?', or should we construe them in some other way? In this chapter, we shall examine the view that ontological questions should not be taken at face value, and that affirmative answers to them do not have the implications we would suppose them to have. On this view, they are not, in other words, about the ultimate nature of reality at all. This position is called *deflationism*. Clearly, if deflationism can be defended, it has significant implications for the ontological question with which this book has been concerned, namely 'Does God exist?'

If ontological questions do not have the meaning we ordinarily ascribe to them, what, according to deflationism, is their meaning? We shall take as our text Rudolf Carnap's influential paper, 'Empiricism, Semantics, and Ontology' (1950), which is the classic statement of deflationism. Carnap introduces a distinction which is intended to capture the two legitimate ways of interpreting ontological questions. He writes:

> Are there properties, classes, numbers, propositions? In order to understand more clearly the nature of these and related problems, it is above all necessary to recognize a fundamental distinction between two kinds of questions concerning the existence or reality of entities. If someone wishes to speak in his language about a new kind of entities, he has to introduce a system of new ways of speaking, subject to new rules; we shall call this procedure the construction of a linguistic *framework* for the new entities in question. And now we must distinguish two kinds of questions of existence: first, questions of the existence of certain entities of the new kind *within the framework*; we shall call them *internal questions*; and second, questions concerning the existence or reality *of the system of entities as a whole*, called *external questions*. Internal questions and possible answers to them are formulated with the help of the new forms of expressions. The answers may be found either by purely logical methods or by empirical methods, depending upon whether the framework is a logical or factual one. An external question is of a problematic character which is in need of closer examination.
>
> (Carnap 1950, p. 242)

Let us go through the argument more slowly. A framework, in the sense being employed here, is a system of terms and expressions together with rules governing those terms and expressions. Consider an example with which Carnap was particularly concerned, the system of numbers. This consists firstly of terms such as 'three', 'five', etc.; the general term 'number'; terms for relations between numbers, such as 'is greater than'; terms for properties of numbers, such as 'prime' and 'negative'; and terms for functions, such as 'plus', 'divided by'. Secondly, the system contains expressions in which those terms occur: 'five is a number', 'three is a prime number'. Thirdly, the system contains rules governing relations between numbers, both of a specific form ('three plus three is six') and a more general form ('the result of multiplying two negative numbers is a positive number').

Having introduced a framework, we can proceed to raise certain questions within it. For example, we can ask, 'Is there a prime number greater than a hundred?' This is an example of an internal question, since it presupposes adoption of the framework of numbers, and the answer to it will be provided by following the rules of that framework.

Now consider the 'metaphysical' question, 'Are there numbers?' How are we to interpret this? Carnap presents us with the following dichotomy. Suppose first that it is intended as an internal question, one which presupposes the framework of numbers. Then the obvious answer is, 'Yes', because the proposition 'There are numbers' follows from more specific internal propositions, such as 'There is a prime number between three and seven'. But the answer to such a question is, of course, quite trivial. Since we have already accepted the framework, we are already talking in terms of numbers, and so, in that unremarkable sense, we have admitted that there are numbers. But if 'Are there numbers?' is not intended as an internal question, it must be interpreted as *external* in nature, i.e. as posed before we agree to adopt the framework. But the only sense we can then give it is to take it as asking whether we should adopt the framework of numbers or not. If so, then the question would appear to be a practical one, concerning the advisability of adopting the framework. The obvious answer to such a question is that numbers are far too useful for us *not* to adopt the framework. If the question is a practical one, however, it cannot be a theoretical one, i.e. one concerning the facts of the matter. Consequently, the answer to it tells one nothing about the reality of numbers.

Carnap's deflationist argument, then, is this. A question such as 'Are there numbers?' can only be interpreted in one of two ways: as an internal question or as an external question. If as an internal question, the answer is trivial. If as an external question, the answer is simply a practical recommendation. Neither answer commits one to the metaphysical reality of numbers, whatever that is supposed to involve. Since, however, there is no other legitimate interpretation of the question, the issue of the reality of numbers is simply a non-issue.

Another example considered by Carnap is that of the system of physical objects:

> Once we have accepted the thing language with its framework for things, we can raise and answer internal questions; e.g., 'Is there a white piece of paper on my desk?', 'Did King Arthur actually live?', 'Are unicorns and centaurs real or merely imaginary?', and the like. These questions are to be answered by empirical investigations... The concept of reality occurring in these internal questions is an empirical, scientific, non-metaphysical concept. To recognize something as a real thing or event means to succeed in incorporating it into the system of things at a particular space–time position so that it fits together

with the other things recognized as real, according to the rules of the framework.

From these questions we must distinguish the external question of the reality of the thing world itself. In contrast to the former questions, this question is raised neither by the man in the street nor by scientists, but only by philosophers. Realists give an affirmative answer, subjective idealists a negative one, and the controversy goes on for centuries without ever being solved. And it cannot be solved because it is framed in the wrong way. To be real in the scientific sense means to be an element of the system; hence this concept cannot be meaningfully applied to the system itself.

(ibid., pp. 242–3)

There remains only the external, practical, interpretation of the question of the reality of things, i.e. 'Should we accept the thing framework?', and an affirmative answer means only that the framework is a useful one. If this does not satisfy the metaphysician, then so much the worse for metaphysics.

The example of physical objects above makes it more clear why Carnap only allows a pragmatic, non-theoretical construal of external questions. When we ask 'Are physical objects *real?*' we are using a term ('real') that can only be defined within a particular framework, at least if we take the question at face value. Obviously the only appropriate framework to appeal to in defining 'real' is, in this context, the physical object framework. It would make no sense at all to ask if physical objects were real in the sense of 'real' as defined in the system of numbers. But if we are using 'real' as it is defined in the physical object framework, then we have already adopted the framework, and the question can only be an internal one. If we intend the question as an external question, then we cannot take it at face value. The only question we can sensibly raise with regard to the framework as a whole is whether or not it is worth our while to accept it.

If Carnap is right, the debate between realism and positivism presented in the previous chapter is simply misguided. His own position is best described as instrumentalism: statements supposedly about certain entities are merely devices useful for the purposes of calculation, prediction, or classification; they are not descriptive of the world and so need not be regarded as either true or false.

We may be bewildered by this. Is Carnap saying that, when I say 'I am sitting at a table', that statement is not capable of being true, or that tables are not real? The best way to read Carnap, I think, is to take him as making this suggestion: instead of asking whether neutrons, or numbers, or natterjack toads, are *real*, which is a question inviting confusion, we should ask the more straightforward question whether it is useful to introduce a language that contains terms such as 'neutron', or 'number', etc. We can certainly retain the words 'true' and 'false', but when I say 'I am sitting at a table', the truth of such a statement just consists in the fact that I have adopted a certain framework and, according to the rules of that framework, I am entitled to say that I am sitting at a table.

## THE ARGUMENT APPLIED TO THEISM

If there is, as Carnap suggests, something suspicious about realism, then doubts can be raised about the traditional debate between theists and atheists. Perhaps, after all, they are not debating an intelligible issue. To see if this conclusion can be drawn from Carnap's argument, let us try to put that argument in a theological context.

We can define the *theistic framework* as follows. First, we introduce the term 'God' and associated expressions: 'God is good', 'God is unique', etc. Second, we introduce expressions linking the term 'God' with the physical object framework: 'God created the universe', 'God loves his creation', etc. Third, we introduce methods for deciding the truth of certain propositions. In part this will consist of an authoritative text, such as the Bible, or the Koran. The framework may also distinguish, among the statements in the text, between those statements which are intended to be read literally, and those that are intended as metaphorical or allegorical.

Now consider the question 'Does God exist?' The deflationist treatment of this question will presumably go as follows. If we construe the question as an internal question, as posed within, say, the Christian theological framework, then the answer is both obvious and trivial, since 'God exists' follows from other internal propositions, such as 'Jesus was the son of God'. If, on the other hand, we construe the question as an external question concerning the advisability of adopting the framework, then we can only give it a pragmatic answer. The pragmatic reason for adopting the theistic framework is that, by adopting it, we are thereby adopting a religious ideal and so are enabled to lead a more fulfilling and perhaps also more ordered life. But this carries no ontological commitment to the reality of God – indeed the deflationist conclusion is that the whole question of whether God is real or not is a pseudo-question, a question we cannot make sense of. What we have here, in effect, is an argument for radical theology, in that the view of theological statements we are left with, if the argument works, is an instrumentalist one:

theological statements do not refer to, or describe, a transcendent being and are not intended to do so.

Before assessing the deflationist argument, we should consider a number of objections to our theological application of it. It might be suggested that, so far from being a natural target for the argument, theistic discourse is quite disanalogous to the kinds of proposition which Carnap wanted to challenge. Here are some disanalogies:

(a) The deflationist argument concerns general questions, of the form 'Are there Fs?' In contrast, the question 'Does God exist?' is not general at all, but particular: it concerns an individual object.

(b) No-one can reasonably refrain from talking about, or using the concept of, numbers. And no-one can seriously suspend belief in physical objects. It is the fact that we cannot avoid operating within such frameworks that we do not make adoption of them conditional on some prior decision as to whether the entities they seem to concern really exist or not. In contrast, the theistic framework is not forced upon us. It is in fact extremely controversial, and acceptance of that framework crucially depends upon a prior acceptance of the ontology of that framework – i.e. a belief in God's existence.

(c) Questions about existence are most problematic when we are dealing with abstract entities, i.e. things that we cannot perceive or, more generally, causally interact with. Such entities include numbers, propositions and classes – the very entities which Carnap highlights in his initial statement of the argument. There is something very suspicious about the notion that numbers or propositions are real, but nothing at all suspicious in the notion that physical objects such as chairs are real. Now God is clearly a concrete entity, not an abstract one, so the argument, we may feel, is not appropriately applied to theism.

How important are these disanalogies? Let us take each of them in turn. In reply to (a), the reason why 'Does God exist?' might be thought to be a particular question is that the term 'God' appears to be used here as a proper name, intended to identify something specific. But if 'God' could *only* be used as a proper name, then the question 'Does God exist?' would presuppose its own answer. And if the term 'God' had no reference, then the question would be devoid of content. Only within the theistic framework can 'God' be used as a proper name, just as the term 'Martin Chuzzlewit' can only be used as a proper name within the context of the novel of that title. We can ask internal questions, such as 'Did God divide the Red Sea?', where 'God' is used as a proper name, since the term is given a reference within the framework. However, if 'Does God exist?' is intended as an external question, then it must be construed as a general question: 'Is there a God?', or, more explicitly, 'Is there an $x$ such that $x$ created the universe, is perfectly good, revealed himself to the chosen people of Israel, etc.?' This question, containing no proper names, is of precisely the same form as 'Are there numbers?' So, if the deflationist argument applies to any general existential question, it applies to the question of God's existence.

As to (b), it is quite true that we can hardly refrain from adopting the framework of numbers, or physical objects. But we can refrain from adopting the framework of neutrons and electrons, and there seems to be no reason why the argument cannot be turned on these highly theoretical entities of physics. The general acceptability of the framework, then, does not seem to play an important role in the deflationist argument.

What, finally, of (c)? It is clear from Carnap's discussion that he is not aiming specifically at abstract objects. In fact, as we saw from one of the quotations above, he deals explicitly with physical objects. He also applies the argument to space–time points (ibid., p. 248). In each case, the structure of the argument is exactly the same. It may well be that we are particularly suspicious of abstract entities, and realism over such entities raises serious epistemological problems, but if the argument is a sound one, then it applies quite generally. In any case, if we are impressed by the problematic nature of abstract objects, it is worth remarking that the properties traditionally ascribed to God, namely being outside space and time, unchanging, and necessarily existent, put him much closer to the category of numbers than that of ordinary physical objects.

I think these considerations show that we are not committing some elementary error in putting Carnap's argument in this theological context. However, as we shall see, this last point, about the peculiarly problematic nature of abstract objects, will turn out to be a crucial one.

## DEFLATIONISM DEFLATED?

Let us rehearse the argument for deflationism before criticising it. A framework is a language plus a set of rules: rules which tell one how the terms of the language are to be used, and rules which tell one how to decide certain questions posed in the language. *Internal* questions are questions that can be raised only when a given framework is adopted. *External* questions are those that can be raised, prior to accepting the framework, about the framework itself. To make this distinction more clear, it may be helpful to employ an analogy with fiction. Take a novel, like *Middlemarch*. This, in effect, is a framework: it introduces the names of certain characters and places, and it provides a means of deciding what is true of those characters and places. Deciding to read the book, to become involved with it, is to adopt a framework. Now suppose, as we read the book, we ask, 'Did Dorothea publish Casaubon's *Key to All Mysteries*?' Since, outside this fiction, 'Dorothea' and 'Casaubon' simply fail to refer, this is a question we can only raise from within the fiction of *Middlemarch*, i.e. the question must be an internal one. Reading the book, we discover the answer to that question.

Deciding to read a book, to engage imaginatively with a fiction, is not to take it as being true. It is only to pretend that it is true, as we suggested in the previous chapter. Similarly, our decision to adopt a framework does not commit us to the existence of entities talked about in that framework, and we are not committed to the ultimate truth of any answer to internal questions. It is only true-in-the-novel that Dorothea married Casaubon. Similarly, it is only true-in-the-framework-of-numbers that there are prime numbers greater than 3. Once we understand this, we realise that ontology, the study of what exists, should be abandoned. When we ask 'Are there Fs?', unless we are posing some unintelligible, unanswerable, metaphysical question, we are either asking an external question ('Would it be useful for us to adopt the F framework?') or an internal question ('Is it true-in-the-F-framework that there are Fs?').

So much, then, for the argument for deflationism. It is a crucial contention of that argument that adopting a framework does not commit us to thinking of it as reflecting reality. If we think about the analogy between frameworks and novels, this seems to be so. But perhaps there are some frameworks which, when we adopt them, compel us to think of them as reflecting reality. This is essentially what Anselm tried to demonstrate in the case of the theistic framework with the ontological argument. For Anselm, to understand the concept of God is to understand that it represents a being greater than which nothing can be conceived. The fool, who denies God's existence, must at least admit that he has this idea of God in his mind, and so that God exists in the understanding at least. But a being who existed in reality would be greater than one who simply existed in the understanding, so if God existed only in the understanding, we could conceive of a greater being, namely one who existed in reality. But God is precisely that greater than which nothing can be conceived, therefore he must exist in reality. We can present Anselm's argument in Carnap's terms like this: if you have understood the terms of the theistic framework, you cannot but take the framework as describing reality. However, as we saw in Chapter 2, Anselm's ontological argument fails.

Nevertheless, there is one framework which we cannot but take as reflecting reality, and that is the framework which is about *us*. Just which framework this is depends on how we see ourselves – as physical objects, or as minds which could exist in a disembodied form, or simply as objects which exist in time. Talk about ourselves is useful: we want to be able to express our feelings, desires and intentions, and we want to be able to describe our past experiences. The usefulness of that talk is why we adopt it. But, it could be argued, adopting such a framework does not commit us to its *truth*. There may, for all we know, be no such thing as the self. However, suppose we ask: 'Who is adopting this framework? Who is talking about the self?' The answer must be: me. So a precondition of being able to adopt the framework of the self is that the framework, at least in part, must reflect reality. (This is one way of presenting Descartes's famous insight that I cannot be deceived into thinking that I exist, for I must exist in order to be deceived.) Adopting the framework of the self, then, *does* involve accepting that framework as reflecting reality. The fact that a particular framework contains us gives that framework its ontological authority. Suppose we think of ourselves as objects existing in time. Then, if we believe that something stands in a certain temporal relation to us, and so, like us, it is a temporal object, then we cannot but think of that object as real. The problem with abstract object frameworks is that they are not defined in terms of the relations they stand in to us, but rather the *lack* of such relations: according to one kind of realism, numbers are objects outside time and space and independent of any mind. That is why we are suspicious of conferring reality upon such frameworks: there is nothing to give them ontological authority. We may adopt the number framework, but that does not compel us to think of numbers as real, because they are not 'one of us', so to speak. What I am suggesting here is that the natural position to adopt is an ontological parochialism, to believe in the existence only of things of our kind, things which exist in time. Consider the question, 'Is *Middlemarch* true?' Anyone asking this is unlikely to be asking a question internal to the novel, because that would be to ask whether the events related in the novel actually take place in the novel, and the answer to that is obvious. The question, if meant seriously, is an external one, the question whether *Middlemarch* corresponds to reality, where 'reality' here is the world in which *we* live. If the answer is 'Yes', this surely commits us to the reality of the characters, places and events related in the novel.

Carnap's approach to ontological questions is most appropriately applied, then, to problematic entities such as numbers. It is not appropriately applied to things like us, objects existing in time. This provides a new twist to the debate about whether God should be thought of as an entity which exists in time or as one which exists outside of time. If he is conceived of as existing in time, then we can give a clear sense to the question 'Does God exist?': we are asking whether he is part of the same framework as us. But if, as some philosophers have urged, the concept of God is that of a being outside of time altogether, then it seems appropriate to class God with numbers and other abstract objects. In other words, 'Does God exist?', like 'Do numbers exist?', would best be treated as a question about the advisability of adopting the theistic framework, and not about the reality of God.

## SUMMARY

'Does God exist?' is an example of an ontological question. Such questions, however, are problematic. What do we mean when we say that something exists? In 'Empiricism, Semantics, and Ontology', Rudolf Carnap argued that such questions can only be made intelligible by construing them either as questions about the advisability of adopting what he called a 'framework', or as questions posed within that framework. His conclusion was that we can accept talk 'about' entities in, for example, mathematics or physics without being obliged either to believe in the reality of such entities, or to provide a reductionist account of them in terms of something else. This is the argument for *deflationism*.

If we take theism as, among other things, a statement of an ontological position, then it faces Carnap's deflationist argument. If his argument goes through, then not only is the issue of the reality of numbers and the like a specious issue, but the question of God's existence is also undermined. In other words, if deflationism is correct, then we should be theological instrumentalists, and hold that theistic statements are non-descriptive.

However, Carnap's argument is most plausible when we consider abstract entities, that is entities which are supposed (by some) to exist outside space and time. It is not so plausible when applied to temporal objects, for we ourselves are temporal objects and we cannot but believe in our own existence. The fundamental meaning of 'exist' is to have a location in time. So 'Does God exist?' should either be seen as a question about whether God exists in time, or should be construed as the deflationist would construe it.

## FURTHER READING

A well-known attack on the meaningfulness of 'metaphysical' and theological questions, not discussed here, is vigorously presented in A.J. Ayer's *Language, Truth and Logic*, London: Gollancz, 1936.

Rudolf Carnap's argument for deflationism is presented in 'Empiricism, Semantics, and Ontology'. This originally appeared in *Revue Internationale de Philosophie* vol. 4 (1950), and was reprinted, with some modifications, in P. Benacerraf and H. Putnam, (eds), *Philosophy of Mathematics*, 2nd Edition, Cambridge: Cambridge University Press, 1983, pp. 241–57.

Descartes's famous argument that we cannot doubt our own existence is stated in the second of his Meditations. See René Descartes, *Discourse on Method and Meditations on First Philosophy*, edited by Donald A. Cress, 3rd Edition, Indianapolis: Hackett Publishing Company, 1993. Far from being universally accepted, the argument has raised a great deal of controversy. For discussion, see, e.g., Georges Dicker, *Descartes: An Analytical and Historical Introduction*, Oxford: Oxford University Press, 1993, Chapter 2.

A conception of God as outside time is defended in Paul Helm's *Eternal God: A Study of God without Time*, Oxford: Clarendon Press, 1988.

# 10 Should the atheist fear death?

If you were to destroy in mankind the belief in immortality, not only love but every living force maintaining the life of the world would at once be dried up.

Fyodor Dostoyevsky, *The Brothers Karamazov*

## RIDDLES OF MORTALITY

We come, finally, to the topic of death. It is here that the contrast between theism and atheism seems at its sharpest. For when we contemplate death, theism can comfort us in both personal and impersonal terms. In personal terms, theism can offer us the hope of eternal life, a better existence beyond death. In impersonal terms, it offers an antidote to our dismay at the transience of all natural things. Everything that we see passes away, but God is eternal and unchanging. And, in so far as those things which are valuable, such as love and goodness, reside in him, these too are eternal. For the atheist, it seems, there is nothing but change and decay.

Not all theists, however, believe in life after death. And some non-theistic religions involve the idea of the immortality of the soul. So the contrast between theism and atheism need not always be quite as sharp as it was presented above. Nevertheless, theists often have a distinctive view of death and transience, a view from which they draw comfort and strength. What resources has the atheist at his disposal when he contemplates the end of all things? In this last chapter, we shall look at some of the reasons why death is dreaded, and consider whether these reasons are good ones.

Death is a temporal phenomenon, in that it is a kind of change, and so takes place in time. Further, many of the puzzles it raises involve aspects of time. Here are some of the most prominent questions:

1 Why do we care more about future non-existence after our death than about *past* non-existence before our birth?

2  Why are we appalled by the attenuation of the effects of our life after we die? Why, for example, do we fear being forgotten and our various projects crumbling to nothing?

3  Why are we repelled by the thought of endless stretches of future time in which the universe is, as the Second Law of Thermodynamics seems to predict, frozen and lifeless?

4  Why, if we are appalled by death, are some of us also (perhaps even more) appalled by its opposite: the infinite extension of our life? Is this not paradoxical, to want to be neither mortal nor immortal?

In what follows, we shall see how these puzzles are informed by a certain picture of time, and what happens when we shift to a different picture.

## THE RIVER OF TIME AND THE SEA OF ICE

In some respects, time seems utterly unlike space, and their dissimilarity goes deeper than the mere fact that time has only one dimension whereas space has three. On the first theory of time we shall present, which I will call the *A-theory*, time consists intrinsically of a past, present and future. Space, in contrast, does *not* consist intrinsically of a 'here' and a 'there'. 'Here' is wherever I happen to be, but that need not be the same place as the place which is 'here' to you. Whatever 'here' denotes depends simply on the location of the speaker. We can put this by saying that the distinction between here and there is relative to a particular position in space. What is remarkable about the present moment, however, is that it seems to be the same for all of us. This is so, for the A-theorist, because when we distinguish between what is present and what is not present, the distinction corresponds to an objective division in time and is not relative to the position in time of the speaker. Even if there were no observers, there would still be a present moment, distinct from past and future moments. But there would be no unique place which was 'here', since the hereness of a place just reflects an observer's perspective. We may, of course, talk of the perspective of an inanimate object and say that its location is 'here' with respect to that object, but we must still admit that 'hereness' is not an intrinsic feature of any place.

There are two variants of the A-theory which take a stance on the reality of past and future. On the first of these, which we might call the *closed past, open future* view, the past is real, the future is not. What this metaphysical statement means is that there are *past* facts, whether or not those facts are in principle accessible to us, but no *future* facts. For example, there is a fact of the matter as to whether or not the last dinosaur (or dinosaurs) suffered from indigestion, whether or not there is any evidence one way or the other. There is, however, as yet no fact of the matter as to whether human beings will colonise Pluto. It may be that some statements we can make about the future are now true, but if they are, they are so only because there are some present facts which guarantee that the statements in question are true. For example, because the Sun can only produce a finite amount of energy before it is finally extinguished, it is inevitable that the Sun will not exist for an infinite amount of time. Conditions being as they are, things cannot turn out otherwise. So that is one truth about the future. But those statements whose truth (or falsity) is not guaranteed by the present state of things are neither true nor false. What will happen is, to a large extent, open.

A more extreme variant of the A-theory is the *open past, open future* view. On this view, neither the future *nor the past* is real: only the present is real. Suppose we ask a question like, 'Did Ethelred the Unready visit (the place we now call) Brighton?' If there is now no trace of such a visit, nor any evidence to show that he never visited Brighton, then it is, on this view, neither true nor false that Ethelred the Unready visited Brighton.

These are the two most familiar versions of the A-theory. It is true that the A-theorist may want to accept the reality of both the past and the future, but since one of the most influential sources of motivation for the A-theory is the belief that the future is not real, we can, I think, ignore this third variant. As for the other two, I suspect that our intuitions oscillate between them. It is quite hard to accept that many statements about the past are neither true nor false. We are much more likely to suppose that there is a fact of the matter with respect to every statement we could make about the past, and that the lack of evidence in certain cases demonstrates no more than our ignorance of those facts. On the other hand, we are drawn to the view that the present is a privileged position and are uncomfortable with the notion that the past is as real as the present. Augustine neatly caught this discomfort when he asked whether there was a 'secret place' to which the past went when it was over. His conclusion was that the past exists only in our memories.

The A-theory is an attempt to capture in precise terms our sense of the passage, or transience, of time. It is, for some, the truth behind the metaphorical picture of the river of time. In striking contrast to this view is the *B-theory*, which altogether denies that time passes and holds that time is much more like space than we generally suppose. For the B-theorist, the division between past, present and future is closely analogous to the division between the spatially local and the distant. A given time is present only with respect to some particular event or observation. Without observers, it would make no sense to talk of a present moment except in the entirely ordinary sense that every time is present with respect to itself, just as every place is local with respect to itself. Past, present and future therefore simply represent our perspective on time, not the intrinsic nature of time itself. What we call the past is simply that series of events which are earlier than the time at which we happen to be talking. The future is simply that series of events which are later than the time at which we are talking. There is no reason to pick out the earlier series of events as more real than the later series of events, any more than we have good reason to think of distant places as unreal, simply because we do not happen to be at them. Consequently, what we call the future is just as real as what we call the present.

If the A-theory can be represented in the picturesque metaphor of the river of time, a suitable metaphor for the B-theory would be the sea of ice, the ninth and last circle of hell as presented in Dante's *Inferno*. In this circle are those who have merited eternal punishment through betraying their benefactors, and all but their heads are submerged in the frozen sea. They provide an image of the world as presented by the B-theory if we think of them as the events which constitute the history of the world. Just as, on the B-theory, events do not move through time by first being future then becoming present and finally receding into the past, so the heads of the damned are fixed in the sea of ice.

This image, however, encourages the thought, often expressed by those hostile to the B-theory, that the B-theorist makes time an illusion. Supporters of the A-theory take time's passage as its essential character-istic and would regard a world without the passage of time as a world without time and change at all. The B-theorist, however, contends that what it is for time to exist is for things to stand in the relations of earlier than, simultaneous with, and later than, other things. My birth, for example, occurred during Harold Macmillan's premiership, was earlier than the assassination of John F. Kennedy and was later than the construction of the Berlin Wall. All that is required for change, according to the B-theory, is that objects have different properties at different times. Suppose we describe this kind of change as a *first-order change*: change in objects. An event is simply a change in the properties of one or more objects. Then to insist that events themselves must change in respect of their pastness, presentness or futurity is to invoke the idea of *second-order change*: changes themselves changing. A-theorists, in effect, hold that without second-order change there can be no first-order change. The B-theorist will simply deny this connection: there is first-order change, but no second-order change.

A further challenge faced by the B-theorist is to explain the arrow, or direction, of time. An important disanalogy between time and space is that, whereas we can, within limits, travel in any direction in space, we cannot, it seems, travel in any direction in time. We cannot visit the past, and we cannot visit the future. It may be said that the future visits us, but then of course it is no longer future, but present. I cannot, at least given the current state of our technology, decide that tomorrow I shall visit the year 2004. Even defenders of the possibility of time-travel concede that there is in ordinary life an arrow of time, and that it is something for builders of time-machines to overcome. Now the A-theorist takes the arrow of time to be of a piece with the passage of time. Where we are in time is something which time itself imposes on us: it is not a matter for our choosing. Since the B-theorist denies the passage of time, this might be thought to be equivalent to the denial that time has a direction. But it is not equivalent. B-theorists think of time as analogous to space in certain crucial respects, but they do not have to think of them as being analogous in *all* respects. Precisely what constitutes the direction of time is not something agreed upon by all B-theorists, but an influential answer is that the direction of time is nothing more than the direction of *causation*. It is a necessary truth, on this account, that causes always precede their effects. We cannot causally affect what happens at times earlier than our actions; we can only affect what happens at times later than our actions. This is why we cannot visit the past, for to do so would be to affect earlier events. Thus we do not need the passage of time to explain the arrow of time.

We can summarise the two theories as follows:

*The A-theory*

Time passes, and the division between past, present and future is an objective feature of time itself: it does not merely reflect our perspective on time (i.e. where in time we happen to be located). There are two variants:

(a)  The closed past, open future view: the past is real, the future not.
(b)  The open past, open future view: neither past nor future is real.

*The B-theory*

Time does not pass, and the division between past, present and future merely reflects our perspective. All times are equally real.

So much, then, for our two theories of time. The A-theory is the one we intuitively adopt, but I hope I have said enough about the B-theory to show that it is at least a viable alternative to our intuitive view. It is time now to return to our first question about death, namely, why we care more about future non-existence after our death than about past non-existence before our birth.

## DEATH IN THE MIRROR

In an often-cited passage, Lucretius makes a point which is sometimes taken to imply that the fear of death is irrational:

> Again, look back and see how the ancient past of everlasting time before we are born has been nothing to us. Nature then shows us this as a mirror of future time after our final death. Does anything appear horrible there, does anything seem sad?
>
> (*de Rerum Natura*, Book 3, quoted in Sorabji 1983, p. 176)

Whether or not Lucretius wanted, by this, to show the irrationality of our fears, it does provoke the thought that, since we are not appalled by the mirror-image of death, namely the fact that we did not exist before our birth (or conception), we should not be appalled when we look at death itself. Let us call this *the mirror-image argument*. It is, at best, incomplete. The fact is that we do, in general, care more about the future than about the past. What is about to happen to us is a more immediate source of concern than what has happened to us. And when we do brood over what has happened to us, it is often in virtue of its implications for what will happen in the future. Now, given this asymmetry of our concerns, it is simply not true that future non-existence will appear to us as nothing more than the mirror-image of past non-existence. But perhaps it ought to appear to us as nothing more than that. So there are two questions. First, what *explains* the asymmetry in our attitudes? Second, is it *rational* to hold on to this asymmetry?

Let us turn first to the A-theory of time for answers to these questions. For the A-theorist, there is an objective difference between past and future, and this is a view of the world reflected by our emotional reactions to events. When an unpleasant, or unfortunate, event is still future, we dread it. When it is past, we feel relief. Death is an unfortunate event, and so, being future, it is something we dread. This goes some way to explaining why we dread future non-existence, but it does not, by itself, rationalise that fear. Perhaps it is only when the event is an unpleasant *experience* that we dread it when it is future and feel relief when it is past. Now non-existence is certainly not an experience. So perhaps it is not to be dreaded?

There is, however, another explanation of why future non-existence is objectively worse than past non-existence, and it has a connection, though rather a subtle one, with the A-theory of time. Let us begin with the consideration that death is bad to the extent that it deprives us of pleasures that we would otherwise have enjoyed. Of course, this implies that death is good to the extent that it saves us from pains that we would otherwise have suffered, but for simplicity let us consider the case where the pleasures that would have been enjoyed outweigh the pains that would have been suffered. Now this does not, by itself, undermine the mirror-image argument, since we can reason as follows: a premature death may be bad, for the reasons given above, but it is no more bad than a late birth. Given that I was born in 1962, the fact (if it is one) that I shall die in 1998 is bad because I am thereby deprived of pleasures that I value. But the reverse of this is equally true: given that I shall die in 1998, the fact that I was not born until 1962 is bad, because had I been born earlier (i.e. had all the events which led up my conception and birth been earlier) I could have had more of the pleasures that I value. A late birth is just as much a depriver of pleasures as a premature death.

Now, of course, we do not ordinarily reason like this. We take our own, or anyone else's, birth date to be fixed, and so see the premature death as the bad thing, not the fact that the birth was as late as it was. Why we do this has, I suggest, to do with the variant of the A-theory that has the greatest hold on our intuitions, namely the closed past, open future view. When I contemplate my birth, I see it as something fixed. It is a fact that I was born in 1962. But when I contemplate my death, I seem to contemplate something not yet fixed. It is not just that I do not know when I shall die but, on the open future view, there is as yet no fact of the matter as to when I shall die. A number of possibilities present themselves, and I naturally prefer those possible futures where I die in old age to those where I die in early middle age. Those possibilities are of more interest to me than the rather abstract possibility that I should have been born in 1952, or 1922. Consequently it does not occur to me to bemoan the fact that I was born when I was, and not earlier. In addition, an early death seems to be objectively bad because it closes off what were genuine possibilities of extended existence, whereas my birth did not close off any genuine possibilities of my having been born earlier.

But now, see what happens when we switch to the B-theory of time. On this view, all times are equally real. What will happen is just as determinate as what has happened. So the date of my death is just as fixed as the date of my birth. I do not mean by this that, by virtue of the present state of things, it is *inevitable* that I shall die in, say, 1998. I may not yet be suffering from any terminal illness. All I mean is that the statement 'I shall die in 1998' is already either true or false. Suppose it is true. Then it is still possible that I should have died in 2038, but only in the rather abstract sense in which it is possible that I should have been born in

1922. A premature death is no more of an evil than a delayed birth. What is bad is simply that my life span is only 36 years rather than 76 years.

So the B-theory undermines one reason to think that future non-existence is more of an evil than past non-existence. It does not, however, undermine the reasonableness of adopting different attitudes to past and future in general. The B-theorist can, in fact, give a very natural explanation of why we are more concerned with the future, by appealing to the account of the direction of time presented in the previous section. The direction of time, it was suggested, consists in the fact that we can only causally affect later events, not earlier ones. We can, therefore, only act to bring about something in the future, not to bring about something in the past. If we are to be effective agents, therefore, we must turn our attention more to the future than to the past. If we spend too much time brooding on the past, rather than planning for the future, we are less likely to be effective agents, since most of our thoughts will be concerned with what, as it turns out, we cannot affect. Natural selection will therefore favour predominantly forward-looking individuals. Our bias towards the future thus has a biological basis.

But is it legitimate to extend this bias to future times after our death? It is rational to be concerned about the future if we can affect it, but if it is rational to care *only* about what we can directly affect, then it is not rational to care about times after our death, since, being dead, we cannot directly affect them. However, we can still *indirectly* affect what happens after our death, by, for example, initiating projects that are carried on by others. Whether it is rational to care about times after our death, therefore, depends largely on what motivates our actions. If we are simply interested in the experienced quality of our lives, and have reason to act only in so far as our actions will improve that quality, then it is not rational to care about those future times when we can have absolutely no experiences whatsoever. Arguably, however, we are interested in rather more than simply the experienced quality of our lives. We are also motivated to do entirely altruistic things, which will improve the quality of *other* people's lives. This is certainly something we can indirectly affect even when we are dead.

It is often suggested, of course, that even apparently purely altruistic behaviour has an element of self-interest in it. We may imagine a prominent benefactor being concerned, not only for the continued welfare of the beneficiaries, but also that he or she should continue to be recognised as the benefactor. No doubt it is a great comfort to think that one's good works will continue after death, but it would remove a considerable layer of icing from the cake to be told that, after death, we would become entirely *incognito*. This takes us to our second question:

why are we appalled by the idea that the effects of our life will, after our death, be rapidly attenuated?

## IMMORTALITY: REAL AND VICARIOUS

In the poem *Ozymandias*, Shelley conjures up the image of a ruined monument to a once great ruler, consisting of little more than 'Two vast and trunkless legs of stone' and a 'shattered visage' lying alone in the desert. We are given no more than a hint of the extent of his dominion:

> And on the pedestal these words appear:
> "My name is Ozymandias, king of kings:
> Look on my works, ye Mighty, and despair!"
> Nothing beside remains. Round the decay
> Of that colossal wreck, boundless and bare
> The lone and level sands stretch far away.

In the context of such complete obliteration, the inscription seems merely pathetic. The fact that there was once a great empire is made less significant, it seems, by its eventual destruction, and the pretensions of its ruler in consequence seem absurd.

The fate of Ozymandias is a reminder of our own: 'Remember thou art dust, and to dust thou shalt return'. It shows that our attempt to achieve a kind of vicarious immortality through our children, books, charitable works, or whatever, may ultimately be frustrated. Why does it matter to us to have such memorials? Why is the thought of being utterly forgotten and reduced to nothing so appalling? Again, it is, I suggest, a particular view of time which is informing our desires and fears, but this time it is the *second* variant of the A-theory, the open past, open future view, which is doing so. On this view, the past is unreal, and what is true about the past is so only by virtue of the traces that now remain of it. The consequence of such a view is that, if there are no traces of a given event which is conjectured to have taken place, then there is simply no fact of the matter as to whether the event took place or not. Thus, the significance of the past is determined entirely from our present perspective. This is not just the trivial truth that what is significant to us now can only be determined from our present perspective, but the more substantial thesis that what is actually true about the past is constituted by present fact. This provides further significance to the activities of those historical revisionists who deny the existence of the Holocaust. If history is rewritten and decisive evidence destroyed, then, on the open past view, it would at some future date *no longer be determinately true* that the Holocaust occurred. This, then, is why we are concerned to live on in the guise of our various productions and projects: to prevent the truth about the past from being obliterated. If all traces of our lives are lost, then we become, in a literal sense, non-persons.

This also provides an answer to our third question. If, at some future time, nothing at all exists, then the truth, not just about us, but about our history and everything we care about, is also lost.

If we are influenced by the open past, open future view, however, then we are not consistent in our application of it. On this view, only the present is real, so what matters is what is the case *now*. My significance should be assessed from my present perspective, not some imagined future one. In laying down our own memorials, we project ourselves in imagination into some future time when we no longer exist (this feat of imagination itself involves some conflict, at least if it involves the image of *ourselves* witnessing our non-existence) and consider our significance from that perspective. But at present, that future time is unreal, and we should accord that future perspective not more significance than our present one, but less significance.

The shift to the B-theory removes all talk of a privileged perspective. If all times are equally real, then, regardless of whether all traces of my life will be destroyed, it will always be the case that I once lived and did various deeds. These truths can never be obliterated, even if the evidence for them is. I have nothing to fear, at least in this respect, from the ravages of time.

But, it might be said, even if we recognise that the past is as real as the present, we may still wish the effects of our life to continue beyond our deaths. This may show how difficult it is to rid ourselves of the A-theory of time, but there is another source of this desire: we measure our significance by the extent of the causal consequences of our actions. The more temporally extended these effects are, the more significant we consider ourselves to be. But, equally, the more *spatially* extended those effects are, the more significant we consider ourselves to be. Hence the desire to affect the lives of many individuals, the desire to have our books read widely, the desire to extend our empires. So our craving for vicarious immortality need not imply any disanalogy between time and space.

We now turn to our final question: why, if we are appalled by death, are we also (perhaps even more) appalled by its opposite: the infinite extension of our life? The answer to this is surely very simple. Most of our pleasures are transient and, though we may often regret their passing, they would cease to be pleasures if they went on and on. We would simply become bored with them. Most of the things we strive for in life are valuable precisely because we only have a limited amount of time to acquire and enjoy them.

It does not follow from this, however, that an infinite life would necessarily be unpleasant. Suppose there are immortal beings who see the world as it really is, and not merely from a limited perspective. Now, if the B-theory of time is the true one, then our ordinary experience of time as a series of transient moments, on which experience the feeling of tedium depends, reflects only our perspective on reality. So, since the immortal beings have no perspective, their experience of time would not be as a series of transient moments. We can barely imagine what experience would be like for them, but it would surely be sufficiently different for eternal life to be for them nothing like the horror it would be for us.

## SUMMARY

If we do not believe that we continue to exist in some disembodied form after death, then the prospect of death may seem appalling. However, our attitude towards death is, to some extent, conditioned by our view of time. According to our ordinary conception of things, based on everyday experience, time flows in the sense that events are for ever receding into the past. Future events assume a greater significance than past ones, and future misfortune seems far worse than past misfortune. Part of this ordinary conception is a view of past and future as less real than the present: the past has gone, and the future has not yet arrived. This implies that, when we are dead, we cease to be part of reality, and our significance is thereby diminished.

In this chapter, we explored the possibility that the ordinary conception of time might be false, that time does not in fact flow, and that all times are equally real. Past, present and future, according to this different view of things, are closely analogous to the distinction between here and there. This view of time lends some support to the suggestion that our future non-existence after our deaths should be nothing more to us than our past non-existence before our births.

There are certain metaphysical conceptions of the world which affect the way we look at things, and the way we see ourselves. I believe that the theory of time, according to which all times are real, is one such conception. For some people, the psychological effects of such an idea are wholly negative ones. If future times are real, it has been argued, then what is to be is already in some sense fixed, and so we are in the grip of fate. But, as I have tried to show in these last pages, this view of time can affect us in positive ways. We need not be dismayed by the apparent transience of everything we value, for, if the passage of time is an illusion, such things are eternally real. And death is no longer the passage into oblivion: it is simply one of the temporal limits of our lives.

At the beginning of this book, we tried to define what religion is. On one view, it is a way of life based on a metaphysical conception of the world. On another view, it is a way of life which is supported by a fictional conception of the world. The atheist, I want to conclude, can have it both ways. The kind of atheism I have defended in this book is not the rejection of all religious thought and language, but rather the rejection of theological realism. The atheist simply does not believe that there is, independently of us, a deity responsible for the creation and order of the world. This is quite compatible with engagement with religious practice as a peculiarly valuable form of make-believe. But, in addition, the atheist may have a metaphysical conception of the way the world really is, a conception which is not given directly in experience, but from which he derives his sense of what matters. To this extent, his metaphysics is a religion.

## FURTHER READING

There is a large number of recent articles and discussions on death. Among the ones which explore the relation between time and death (including the mirror argument) are: Thomas Nagel, 'Death', *Nous* 4 (1970), pp. 73–80, reprinted, with alterations, in *Mortal Questions*, Cambridge: Cambridge University Press, 1979; Richard Sorabji, *Time, Creation and the Continuum*, London: Duckworth, 1983, Chapter 12; Fred Feldman, 'Some Puzzles about the Evil of Death', *Philosophical Review* 100 (1991), pp. 205–27; Piers Benn, 'My Own Death', *The Monist* 76 (1993), pp. 235–51. The last of these makes explicit use of the B-theory of time.

St Augustine's *Confessions* provides a fascinating introduction to problems of time. It is readily available in R.S. Pinecoffin's translation, Harmondsworth: Penguin, 1961. On p. 267 of this edition, we find what is essentially a statement of the open past, open future view. For an introductory discussion of the A-theory and the B-theory see Robin Le Poidevin and Murray MacBeath (eds), *The Philosophy of Time*, Oxford: Oxford University Press, 1993, pp. 1–5; and for the problem of the direction of time, ibid. pp. 6–9. Hugh Mellor's *Real Time*, Cambridge: Cambridge University Press, 1981 is an extended defence of the B-theory, and Quentin Smith's *Language and Time*, New York: Oxford University Press, 1993, is both an extended attack on the B-theory, and a defence of a rather unusual form of the A-theory.

# Glossary

**A-theory:** A theory of time according to which time passes, and the distinction between past, present and future reflects an objective feature of time itself, not merely our perspective on time.

**Analytic:** A proposition is analytically true if its negation (q.v.) is self-contradictory. (*See also:* Necessary)

**Anthropic principle:** Broadly, a principle which explains the laws of nature or fundamental constants (q.v.) being as they are in terms of the existence of observers. The *weak anthropic principle* states that what we can expect to observe must be restricted by the conditions necessary for our presence as observers. The *strong anthropic principle* states that the universe had to be such as to permit the emergence of observers in it at some stage. The strong, but not the weak, principle, is an example of teleological explanation (q.v.).

*A priori:* A proposition can be known to be true (or false) *a priori* if and only if it is possible to discover whether or not it is true without recourse to experience.

**B-theory:** A theory of time according to which time does not pass, and the distinction between past, present and future merely reflects our perspective on time.

**Causal reductionism:** In this book, the doctrine that teleological explanation (q.v.) is a way of drawing attention to causal relations in the world, and that in the absence of causal relations, teleological explanation is inappropriate.

**Chance:** The likelihood of a certain outcome, such as a coin's landing heads, measured by values between 0 and 1. A value of 0 indicates that the event cannot happen, 1 that it must happen. (*See:* Frequency theory and Propensity theory)

**Closed time:** Time is closed if and only if it is both finite and has neither a beginning nor an end.

**Compatibilism:** The view that determinism (q.v.) is compatible with human freedom. (*See also:* Negative freedom)

**Contingent:** The existence of something is contingent if and only if it is possible that it could not have existed. A proposition is contingently true if and only if it is possible for it to be false. (*See also:* Necessary)

**Cosmological argument:** An argument (or arguments) for the existence of God which typically has as one of its premises the proposition that things of a certain kind must have causes for their existence, and as another premise the proposition that the universe is an entity of that kind. The *temporal argument* argues from the premise that the universe has a beginning, the *modal argument* from the premise that the universe is contingent (q.v.). Other forms of cosmological argument point to a certain feature of the universe, such as the fact that it is continually changing, and argue that something must be the cause of that feature.

**Deflationism:** The view that ontological questions (q.v.) are not to be taken at face value, but should be reconstrued as questions about the usefulness of adopting a certain language.

**Descriptive goodness:** An action $x$ is descriptively good for $y$ if and only if doing $x$ would be beneficial to $y$, or would help to satisfy $y$'s desires.

**Determinism:** The universe is deterministic if and only if, given the laws of nature and the state of the universe at a particular time, only one history of the universe is possible.

**Emotivism:** The view that moral judgements merely reflect our feelings, rather than describe some intrinsic feature of an action. (*See also:* Moral realism)

**Frequency theory:** A theory of chance (q.v.) according to which the chance of an outcome is nothing more than the frequency of that outcome in a certain specified population. (*See also:* Propensity theory)

**Fundamental constants:** Values which play a basic role in physics and which remain the same in all places and at all times. Examples: the speed of light, the charge on an electron.

**Incompatibilism:** The view that determinism (q.v.) is incompatible with human freedom.

**Instrumentalism:** Instrumentalism with respect to statements of a certain kind holds that those statements are non-descriptive, and so are neither true nor false. *Epistemological instrumentalism* is a weaker position, which holds that we can adopt, say, a scientific theory as a useful device, without having to suppose it to be true. (*See also:* Realism and Positivism)

**Libertarianism:** A form of incompatibilism (q.v.), in which it is held that determinism (q.v.) is false and that human agents are not caused by antecedent events to act as they do.

**Meta-ethical argument for atheism:** The meta-ethical argument for atheism presented in this book argues that the following theistic doctrines are inconsistent: (a) The existence of moral values depends on God; (b) 'God is good' is morally significant.

**Meta-ethics:** Sometimes called second-order ethics. The study of the more theoretical aspects of ethics, such as the status of ethical judgements, whether moral values are objective, the relation between moral properties and natural properties.

**Modal realism:** The doctrine that other possible worlds (q.v.) are just as real and concrete as the actual world.

**Moral argument:** An argument for the existence of God based on the existence of moral values.

**Moral explanation:** The moral explanation of the laws of nature is that they are there so as to permit the emergence of moral agents in the universe.

**Moral realism:** The view that moral values exist independently of any human judgement. (*See also:* Emotivism, Moral subjectivism)

**Moral subjectivism:** The view that the moral properties of certain things are just dispositions in those things to cause certain moral reactions in us.

**Necessary:** A proposition is necessarily true if and only if it is not possible for it to be false. (*See also:* Analytic, Contingent)

**Negation:** The negation of any proposition is formed by prefacing that proposition with 'It is not the case that . . . '. Thus 'It is not the case that it is raining' (or, more simply 'It is not raining') is the negation of 'It is raining'.

**Negative freedom:** We are free in a negative sense if we act in the absence of constraint, so that what determines our actions are primarily our desires and beliefs. It is this sense of freedom which compatibilism holds is compatible with determinism (q.v.).

**Non-theistic religion:** A religion which does not posit the existence of a God.

**Ontological argument:** An argument for God which attempts to show that the content of the idea of God (or the definition of 'God') necessitates the actual existence of God.

**Ontological questions:** General questions of a philosophical nature concerning the existence of certain kinds of entities. Examples: 'Are there physical objects?' and 'Are there numbers?'

**Personal explanation:** Explanation in terms of the intentions of an agent.

**Positivism:** Positivism with respect to statements of a certain kind holds that those statements are, or are reducible to, statements about our observations. (*See also:* Instrumentalism, Realism)

**Possible world:** A possible world is a way things could have been. 'The actual world' denotes everything that exists or is the case. It is a matter of controversy whether possible worlds are just abstract representations, like consistent fictions, or real things existing in their own right. (*See also:* Modal realism)

**Prescriptive goodness:** An action $x$ is prescriptively good for one if one ought to perform $x$, independently of one's desires. (*See also:* Descriptive goodness)

**Propensity theory:** A theory of chance (q.v.) according to which the chance of an outcome in a given set of circumstances is constituted by a propensity or disposition of those circumstances to produce that outcome.

**Realism:** Realism with respect to statements of a certain kind holds that those statements are true or false by virtue of the way the world is, independently of our means of discovering whether they are true or false. (*See also:* Instrumentalism, Positivism)

**Relativism:** The view which holds that the truth of a statement is relative to a context. The rejection of absolute truth.

**Scepticism:** Doubt about whether it is possible to know (or, more narrowly, to demonstrate) anything.

**Statistical probability:** *See:* Chance.

**Supervenience:** F-type properties supervene on G-type properties if and only if two things cannot differ in their F-type properties without differing in their G-type properties (or, alternatively, a thing cannot alter in its F-type properties without altering in its G-type properties). For example, the moral properties of an action are sometimes said to supervene on certain of the natural (i.e. non-moral) properties of that action.

**Synthetic:** A proposition is synthetic if and only if it is not analytic (q.v.).

**Teleological argument:** An argument for God which appeals to the notion of purpose. Two important forms are: the analogical argument, which draws an analogy between natural (especially living) objects and human artefacts; and the probabilistic argument, which appeals to the idea that the permutation of features of the universe which were essential for the emergence of life would have been very improbable if there had been no creator.

**Teleological explanation:** Explanation of something in terms of its purpose, function or goal. Examples: 'She runs in order to get fit', 'The outer tissue is rigid in order to avoid rupture of the stem.'

**Theism:** In its most minimal form, the hypothesis that there is a creator of the universe. Traditional forms of theism have also ascribed omnipotence, omniscience, perfect goodness and benevolence to the creator. *Theistic discourse* consists of statements which assume, or appear to assume, the truth of theism.

**Validity:** An argument is valid if and only if it is not possible for the premise(s) to be true and the conclusion false.

# Bibliography

Adams, M.McC. and Adams, R.M. (eds) (1990) *The Problem of Evil* , Oxford: Oxford University Press.

Augustine, St (398) *Confessions*, trans. R.S. Pinecoffin, Harmondsworth: Penguin, 1961.

Ayer, A.J. (1936) *Language, Truth and Logic*, London: Gollancz.

Barnes, J. (1972) *The Ontological Argument*, London: Macmillan.

Benn, P. (1993) 'My Own Death', *The Monist* 76, pp. 235–51.

Braithwaite, R.B. (1955) 'An Empiricist's View of the Nature of Religious Belief', reprinted in Mitchell (1971), pp. 72–91.

Carnap, R. (1950) 'Empiricism, Semantics, and Ontology', reprinted in P. Benacerraf and H. Putnam (eds), *Philosophy of Mathematics*, 2nd Edition, Cambridge: Cambridge University Press, 1983, pp. 241–57.

Charlton, W. (1970) *Aristotle's Physics Books I and II*, Oxford: Clarendon Press.

Craig, W.L. (1979) *The Kalam Cosmological Argument*, London: Macmillan.

—— (1980) *The Cosmological Argument from Plato to Leibniz*, London: Macmillan.

—— and Smith, Q. (1993) *Theism, Atheism and Big Bang Cosmology*, Oxford: Clarendon Press.

Cupitt, D. (1976) *The Leap of Reason*, London: SCM Press

—— (1980) *Taking Leave of God*, London: SCM Press

—— (1984) *The Sea of Faith*, London: BBC Publications.

—— (1995) *The Last Philosophy*, London: SCM Press.

Davies, B. (1993) *An Introduction to the Philosophy of Religion*, 2nd Edition, Oxford: Oxford University Press.

Davies, P.C.W. (1982) *The Accidental Universe*, Cambridge: Cambridge University Press.

Dawkins, R. (1989) *The Selfish Gene*, 2nd Edition, Oxford: Oxford University Press.

Descartes, R. (1641) *Discourse on Method and Meditations on First Philosophy*, ed. Donald A. Cress, 3rd Edition, Indianapolis: Hackett Publishing Company, 1993.

Dicker, G. (1993) *Descartes: An Analytical and Historical Introduction*, Oxford: Oxford University Press.

Feldman, F. (1991) 'Some Puzzles about the Evil of Death', *Philosophical Review* 100, pp. 205–27.

Frankena, W.K. (1973) 'Is Morality Logically Dependent on Religion?', in Helm (1981), pp. 14–33.

Gale, R.M. (1991) *On the Nature and Existence of God*, New York: Cambridge University Press.

Helm, P. (1988) *Eternal God: A Study of God without Time*, Oxford: Clarendon Press.

Helm, P. (ed.) (1981) *Divine Commands and Morality*, Oxford: Oxford University Press.

Hick, J. and McGill, A.C. (eds) (1968) *The Many-faced Argument: Recent Studies on the Ontological Argument for the Existence of God*, London: Macmillan.

Hume, D. (1777) *Enquiry Concerning the Principles of Morals*, edited by L.A. Selby-Bigge, 3rd Edition rev. P.H. Nidditch, Oxford: Clarendon Press, 1975.

—— (1779) *Dialogues Concerning Natural Religion*, ed. J.C.A. Gaskin, Oxford: Oxford University Press, 1993.

Kenny, A. (1979) *The God of the Philosophers*, Oxford: Oxford University Press.

—— (1985) *A Path from Rome*, Oxford: Oxford University Press.

Le Poidevin, R. (1991) 'Creation in a Closed Universe *or*, Have Physicists Disproved the Existence of God?', *Religious Studies* 27, pp. 39–48.

—— and MacBeath, M., (eds) (1993) *The Philosophy of Time*, Oxford: Oxford University Press.

Lear, J. (1988) *Aristotle: The Desire to Understand*, Cambridge: Cambridge University Press.

Leibniz, G.W. (1697) 'On the Ultimate Origination of Things', in *G.W. Leibniz, Philosophical Writings*, ed. G.H.R. Parkinson, London: J.M. Dent, 1973, pp. 136–44.

Leslie, J. (1978) 'Efforts to explain all existence', *Mind* 87, pp. 181–94.

—— (1979) *Value and Existence*, Oxford: Blackwell.

—— (1989) *Universes*, New York: Routledge.

Lewis, D. (1986) *On the Plurality of Worlds*, Oxford: Blackwell.

Mackie, J.L. (1974) *The Cement of the Universe*, Oxford: Clarendon Press.

—— (1977) *Ethics: Inventing Right and Wrong*, Harmondsworth: Penguin.

—— (1982) *The Miracle of Theism*, Oxford: Oxford University Press.

Mellor, D.H. (1969) 'God and Probability', *Religious Studies* 5, pp. 223–34.

—— (1971) *The Matter of Chance*, Cambridge: Cambridge University Press.

—— (1981) *Real Time*, Cambridge: Cambridge University Press.

Mitchell, B. (ed.) (1971) *The Philosophy of Religion*, Oxford: Oxford University Press.

—— (1973)*The Justification of Religious Belief*, London: Macmillan.

Monod, J. (1970) *Chance and Necessity*, trans. Austryn Wainhouse, Glasgow: William Collins, 1972.

Nagel, T. (1970) 'Death', *Nous* 4, pp. 73–80. Reprinted, with alterations, in *Mortal Questions*, Cambridge: Cambridge University Press, 1979.

Newton-Smith, W.H. (1980) *The Structure of Time*, London: Routledge & Kegan Paul.

—— (1981) *The Rationality of Science*, London: Routledge & Kegan Paul.

Pegis, A.C. (ed.) (1945) *The Basic Writings of Saint Thomas Aquinas*, New York: Random House.

Phillips, D.Z. (1965) *The Concept of Prayer*, London: Routledge & Kegan Paul.

—— (1976) *Religion Without Explanation*, Oxford: Basil Blackwell.

Plantinga, A. (1974) *The Nature of Necessity*, Oxford: Clarendon Press.

Read, S. (1994) *Thinking About Logic*, Oxford: Oxford University Press.

Robinson, J.A.T. (1963) *Honest to God*, London: SCM Press.

Rowe, W.L. (1975) *The Cosmological Argument*, Princeton: Princeton University Press.

—— (1978) *Philosophy of Religion: An Introduction*, Belmont: Wadsworth Publishing Company.

Ruben, D-H. (1990) *Explaining Explanation*, London: Routledge.

Russell, B. (1927) 'Why I am not a Christian', in *Why I am not a Christian, and Other Essays*, London: George Allen & Unwin, 1957.

Schlesinger, G. (1984) 'Possible Worlds and the Mystery of Existence', *Ratio* 26, pp. 1–17.

Smith, Q. (1993) *Language and Time*, New York: Oxford University Press.

Sorabji, R. (1983) *Time, Creation and the Continuum*, London: Duckworth.

Storr, A. (1970) *Human Aggression*, Harmondsworth: Penguin.

Swinburne, R. (1979) *The Existence of God*, Oxford: Clarendon Press.

Tredennick, H. and Tarrant, H. (eds) (1993) *Plato, The Last Days of Socrates*, Harmondsworth: Penguin.

van Fraassen, B. (1980) *The Scientific Image*, Oxford: Clarendon Press.

Walton, K. (1978) 'Fearing Fictions', *Journal of Philosophy* 65, pp. 5–27.

—— (1978) 'How Close are Fictional Worlds to the Real World?', *Journal of Aesthetics and Art Criticism* 37, pp. 11–23.

Watson, G. (ed.) (1982) *Free Will*, Oxford: Oxford University Press.

# Index

DATE DUE

MAY 15 2001

JUN 25 2001

DEMCO, INC. 38-2971

The American University

WITHDRAWN AMERICAN UNIV LIB

3 1194 005 557 214